Snapshots

Snapshots

Istantanee

CLAUDIO MAGRIS

TRANSLATED FROM THE ITALIAN

BY ANNE MILANO APPEL

YALE UNIVERSITY PRESS ■ NEW HAVEN & LONDON

A MARGELLOS
WORLD REPUBLIC OF LETTERS BOOK

The Margellos World Republic of Letters is dedicated to making literary works from around the globe available in English through translation. It brings to the English-speaking world the work of leading poets, novelists, essayists, philosophers, and playwrights from Europe, Latin America, Africa, Asia, and the Middle East to stimulate international discourse and creative exchange.

Yale University Press books may be purchased in quantity for educational, business, or promotional use. For information, please e-mail sales.press@yale.edu (U.S. office) or sales@yaleup.co.uk (U.K. office).

Set in Electra and Nobel types by Tseng Information Systems, Inc., Durham, North Carolina. Printed in the United States of America.

Library of Congress Control Number: 2018948421
ISBN 978-0-300-21849-7 (paper : alk. paper)

A catalogue record for this book is available from the British Library.

This paper meets the requirements of ANSI/NISO Z39.48-1992 (Permanence of Paper).

10 9 8 7 6 5 4 3 2 1

To my father and mother

Snapshot

. . . taken with a very short exposure time without the use of a tripod . . .

—Salvatore Battaglia, *Grande dizionario della lingua italiana*

CONTENTS

Snapshots

THE DOVE AND THE TWO-HEADED EAGLE

In the Public Garden of Trieste, at the foot of a statue portraying a nearly naked Italy with a two-headed eagle on her shoulders—symbol of Habsburg Austria vanquished in World War I and transformed into a kind of delicious wild game to be put into a pan—lies a dead dove. It is stretched out, legs in the air, one eye swollen with clotted blood and half hanging out of the socket. Six or seven pigeons emerge from a bush, hop over in an orderly row. They take turns leaping onto the dove, one after another, while the rest of the gang watches; they mount her, frantically flapping their wings, opening and closing their beaks repeatedly. Each time the necrophiliac rape is over quickly; obviously pigeons are speedy lovers—on the other hand, some get back in line and after a few seconds, when it's their turn again, repeat the operation. There are a few pigeons who, before dismounting the increasingly crumpled, shapeless body, stretch their necks out and bend down to give the lifeless, trampled head a couple of violent pecks, striking the injured eye in particular and further reducing it to a pulp. After a few minutes, the gang moves off, disappearing among the pansies. One pigeon remains behind, stops and stares warily, eye dilated, rigid as that of the corpse.

April 17, 1999

THE INNKEEPER AND HIS WAR

Even in the taverns there's talk about the war in Serbia and, by
extension, war in general. The innkeeper behind the bar of a tavern at the foot of San Giusto Hill, in Trieste, also has something to
say. He too had been to war, in '44–'45, but he couldn't really say
for whom and against whom. The Germans had captured him, and
after a few months in prison he had been offered the choice of being
deported to Germany or collaborating with them. After choosing
the second option—you can only choose the lesser evil, he says,
never the greater—he had been assigned to monitor a railway track,
with a Roman butcher, among others, who had taught him the correct temperature at which different salamis must be kept.

Nothing had happened along that track, except that one time
he had helped a woman dragging a very heavy suitcase to cross the
rails and go up the steep escarpment on the other side. In the evenings, however, partisans sometimes showed up and started shooting at the barracks where they were stationed, which was actually
an *osmiza*, a house-tavern on the Karst.[1] Fortunately, the butcher
had a machine gun, which fired many rounds, while the innkeeper
threw a few hand grenades from the window, but blindly, standing
back in the room so as not to make himself a target and not seeing
where the grenades landed. Toward morning when the partisans
withdrew, they would cook themselves something to eat and sleep

for a couple of hours. Captured by the partisans, who in the end had seized the barracks-osmiza, and taken handcuffed to a command in Slovenia, the innkeeper had been recognized in the village by the woman he had helped cross the tracks; released, he had been enlisted by the partisans, who had made him work in their kitchen, where he had even learned the basic rudiments of his future job.

He is a bighearted man with an instinctive sense of solidarity with others. He had sent the largest wreath to the solemn funeral service held in the cathedral of San Giusto in February 1994 for the three RAI journalists killed in Mostar, though he had never met them. Simply out of generosity: "I can't offer them a drink, so . . ." When I ask him if anyone had died during the assaults on that house in which the Germans had stationed them, he replies, "Nooo!" surprised by the question. But he wouldn't have been shocked if it had happened either, maybe to him. Dying is part of the obvious risks of the business of living. In the words of the Polish writer Stanisław Lec—whom he hasn't read, but with whom he certainly agrees fully, without knowing it—living is dangerous no matter what; he who lives dies.

May 5, 1999

UNRELIABLE DEATH

In a room packed with people, in Budapest, a literary conference is under way. At some point alarmed voices can be heard among the crowd, calling for a doctor. An old man, dressed in a blue suit and a white shirt with a stiff collar, has slumped, ashen and lifeless, on a chair. Windows are opened, someone calls an ambulance, the man is carried into an adjoining room and laid on a couch. On the podium, organizers and speakers exchange embarrassed glances, not knowing what to do, torn between respect for life — or rather for (possible) death — and duty toward the public, the instinctive urge to complete something started no matter what, the narcissistic desire to hear one's own book praised; and for each the fear, should the worst happen right when he is speaking, of being viewed as a jinx. Some probably hope that if it really must happen it not happen there but somewhere else, in the hospital, preferably the following day.

Reassuring but cautious word coming from the other room, progressively more positive, leads to a resumption of the talks, which, after some awkwardness, proceed more and more smoothly and brilliantly and end with predictable satisfaction. After the conference, a rich, delectable buffet awaits in another salon, which in a few minutes turns into a crush of people gorging themselves heartily. Suddenly spotted in the midst of the mob is the elderly man, apparently moribund just a short while before, who has fully recovered—probably from a drop in blood sugar—and is stuffing himself with *palacinke* and sausage as he stands there, jostled by the crowd, hands juggling glasses and paper plates.

One of the lecturers looks at him, frowning, perhaps indignant that his reading should have been interrupted by a trifling indisposition; to justifiably interrupt a writer like him requires a serious reason, such as something that actually has to do with death or at least its possibility, not a trivial disruption, unequal to the importance and weight of his books. Death should not be so unreliable. However, you can't arouse people's pity twice in a short period of time; if the old man were to die now, with that chocolate cake in his hands, it would move people much less than two hours earlier. Even for a famous person it would have been quite a misfortune to die shortly after Versace and Princess Diana, when the heart's orgy of mushy sentimentality had for some time depleted the reserves of lachrymal fluid.

June 14, 1999

THIRTEENTHOUSANDEIGHTHUNDREDSEVENTYNINE EVENINGS

The German banker Hilmar Kopper leaves his wife, Irene, after thirty-eight years of marriage, to be with Brigitte Seebacher, the widow of Willy Brandt. There would be nothing to say about it, if the banker, chairman of Deutsche Bank's supervisory board, had not furnished an unintentionally hilarious justification of why he deserted the conjugal roof: instead of keeping his mouth shut—since it's his business and his wife's—or, at most, saying that attraction between him and his wife Irene is over, the way even intense, long-lasting relationships may and sometimes do end, and that one must face the consequences, he proclaims, "I want to do what I want and be free at last. And if I don't feel like eating in the evening, I don't want to have to eat."

Poor chairman, what a miserable life he must have led until now, if he waited thirty-eight years to speak up, if for 13,879 evenings he acquiesced to swallowing mouthfuls of food that stuck in his craw. One can only hope that he is more resolute in his banking operations, of great responsibility. If his wife Irene was such a scourge, the chairman must not have been very well versed in women and love if he didn't notice it in time. He must have been even less experienced if she was not, and he is unable to see the adventure, the freedom, the gamble, the risk, the intensity of a shared life, the loving intimacy that grows ever deeper, the odyssey of living, sleeping, growing old, and especially discovering and loving the world together. The inexperienced chairman obviously does not know how to share such a life without obeying and, seeing himself suddenly free, stamps his feet like a child and repeats, I want, I want, I want! But what makes him think that Brigitte Seebacher won't also force-feed him, given how submissive he is?

The woman's soap-opera statements about love at first sight and life, which of course is beautiful, aren't very promising. Yet Brigitte Seebacher was the wife of Brandt, the man who fought the Nazis and knelt in the Warsaw Ghetto . . . As Baudelaire writes in *Fleurs du mal*, speaking of Andromache, widow of the Trojan hero Hector, about her life as a captive and exile after the fall of Troy and her new relationship with the modest Helenus: "Veuve d'Hector, hélas! et femme d'Hélénus!"[2]

July 19, 1999

AT THE CASTELLI GALLERY

New York, October 1989, at the gallery of Leo Castelli at 420 West Broadway, one of the hubs and sacred places of art from around the world. The gallery that discovered, promoted, and at times created Pop art and in general some of the major schools and trends of contemporary art. It is a somewhat special day; the gallery—like many others in the city—is draped in mourning in protest against the ruling of a judge who sentenced an artist, or perhaps an exhibition or a performance, on charges of obscenity. The paintings on the walls—the works that cultured visitors come from the most diverse parts of the world to see and which they approach as though they were objects of worship—are covered by a black cloth; countless squares and rectangles hang on the walls, concealed by the same black shroud, all alike except for their size. The gallery is obviously empty; its visitors do not usually arrive there unprepared but are generally well informed about what is happening in that temple of postmodernism and every possible "post"-anything; so they are aware that the paintings will not be on view that day.

Sitting on a sofa, Marisa and I chat with Castelli. He is amiable, paternal, and kind, with a trace of melancholy in his comportment reminiscent of a grand gentleman of old Europe; perhaps it is because he is so deeply rooted in centuries-old cultural memory—being a Triestine Jew of multinational ancestry who became a king in New York—that he has been able to sniff out, discover, encourage, guide, and impose the New, a New at times disconcerting and antithetical to the ancient civilization that he embodies down to his calm manner and facial features. Ileana Sonnabend, his former wife and eternal great friend who initiated him into art and the art market and whom we go to greet, is also a fascinating personal symbiosis of old Mitteleuropa and the vast world in which the future is erupting. We speak about Trieste, about mutual friends, books, children, our favorite cafés in various cities.

At a certain point a young woman, a visitor, enters. Unaware of the protest, she thinks she is viewing an exhibition, perhaps the prospect of a new school of painting. She stops in front of each painting—that is, in front of each black cloth—steps back, then moves in for a closer look, sits down, and diligently takes notes; this new painting seems to please and convince her. Castelli glances at me with a hint of embarrassment for a moment, then we go back to talking about old times, while the visitor continues her discovery of a new artistic trend.

September 12, 1999

BE WITH OR GO WITH?

From the terrace you can see the whole city, its lights in the wine-black night, the gentle curved shapes of cupolas and hills in the womb of darkness. The small talk, at tables set properly for a momentous dinner, is lost in the clink of glasses and cutlery, drifting in an indistinct murmur; words and voices are interchangeable, everyone's and no one's, stories that happened to the person sitting beside you but that could very well have happened to the guest in front of you, a hum that fades out like a pleasant, inconsequential rustling. Dinners of a certain tone are a sacred performance, a medieval Mystery play that enacts the unmemorable insignificance of us all. Each of us could take the place of another or be another; behind the mask of the social role, the face lined by the years is more or less the same; in front of a cocktail men and women are all alike, as they are before love and death, destiny's recruits lined up in their uniforms.

"Oh yes," the woman next to me says to someone, "it must have happened when I was with Federico." So the woman with the upswept black hair and gentle eyes, common in myopic individuals, is one of those people, men or women, who "are with," a sad, fatal verb. Among the things that distinguish the love life of human beings is also the modest though not insignificant difference between those who are inclined to "go with" and others instead to "be with." The first has a moral dignity that looms large over the second.

To "go with" is frank, honest Eros, which does not make false promises to be lasting, either to oneself or to others, and does not claim to share the good and bad of life—as if it were a marriage or a complete, deep, lifelong union—and because of this forthright lack of illusion can also offer tenderness, affection, and friendship that will last beyond the brief encounter.

To "be with" on the other hand is often a self-deceptive parody of marriage that involves sharing a life for six months or a year but with all the obligations and rules of marriage: mutual fidelity pro tempore, being a steady couple who must be invited as one, living together, temporary relatives including fathers- and mothers-in-law, sad albeit sincere pretense of being one single flesh, inability to live alone. To "be with" is very different from rebuilding a life or establishing a new romantic union after the failure or at least the end of an earlier one, dissolved by lack of understanding, by death, by incompatibility, or by diminished affection. To "be with" involves the conscious and unconscious planning of many successive mini-marriages, envisaged a priori.

The woman beside me has a nice face, warm and audacious; her mouth does not have that bitter crease etched by aggressive arrogance or that off-putting hardness often sculpted, in certain social classes, by custom and above all by the desire to stress inclusion in the upper echelons. With that face, which one senses is capable of passion and tenderness, the woman deserves a true companion or a lover for one night, rather than a fiancé, as people generally say when they "are with" someone, resorting to a word that, as a prelude to the marriages of one time, already sounded somewhat inane.

December 3, 1999

(OPEN?) COUPLE AT THE CONFERENCE

Valid for two. Often an invitation to a conference extends hospitality in a distinguished hotel, dutifully offered to the more or less illustrious speaker, to a person who might accompany him or her. At one time this invitation presupposed the marital bond between the one called to break the bread of science and the one the speaker wished to bring along; those taking advantage of it were lawful spouses, most often wives or, rarely, husbands, given the majority of men that, up until a few years ago, made up the intellectual class.

Now this male dominance no longer exists or occurs much less frequently; in certain sectors of cultural activity the relationship has at times been overturned, and it is often men who act as parasites or appendages; moreover, they will soon be forced to earn the room in the deluxe hotel and the sophisticated (though for the most part flavorless) official dinners with some collateral activity or initiative aimed at livening up the breaks between the talks and sessions, a task that at one time, on such occasions—especially at medical conferences—was performed by doctors' wives, the most willing and enterprising among the accompanying groups. Human progress has emancipated society from the absurd binding chain linking two nights' lodging and six meals with the matrimonial sacrament or contract; appropriately no conference office staff any longer asks if the woman or man whom the speaker drags along has first gone before a priest in a stole or a mayor's deputy with a tricolor band.

Actually it's hard to see what marriage has to do with a food extravaganza or a gala evening. It is justifiably legitimate to bring along a companion, male or female, a category, moreover, that has become more and more numerous and is destined to numerically outpace that of the married couples. Further progress—whose fate, for that matter, is the impetus to move forward and not backward, as the word itself implies—has abolished the tacit, conventional obligation of gender difference between official participants and those accompanying them; a male presenter can bring either a woman or a man with him, and the same applies for a female speaker. Here progress is real and undeniable since the demise of discrimination against homosexuality has liberated or is liberating humanity from suffering and cruel exclusions.

For those who are not fond of taboos, however, one more step perhaps needs to be taken. Whether spouses or partners of heterosexual, or homosexual, couples, the accompanying individuals seem in any case to have a residual duty to be worthy of the hospitality—namely, that of sharing the bed of the speaker or presenter. No one, of course, explicitly requires it, but the tacit assumption is that there be a sexual bond between the speaker and the one who accompanies him or her. A decent person, respectful of social conventions, at one time officially brought along only a lawful spouse and now shows up with anyone as long as he or she is a bedmate and—tacitly or not, though without a shadow of a doubt—considered such. A friend who works for a major bank in an important position tells me that when the bank organizes a conference and managers receive an invitation that also includes the spouse, if she, as a single woman, inquires about bringing someone, she is regretfully asked if he is her partner, in which case there are no objections.

But why, given that a dinner or a concert has nothing to do with marriage—or with sex either—why this restriction and conventional formality, no less discriminatory and invasive of privacy than the hospitality strictly limited to legitimate spouses was? Why shouldn't someone be able to bring along a cousin with whom he is happy to chat, a schoolmate or tavern buddy, a former fellow soldier from military service, a neighbor whom he or she likes, the corner newsagent, the cashier at the bar with whom he gladly jokes but with whom he has no desire to go to bed, a parish priest who has lively and curious stories to tell about missions in Africa, or anyone else he may wish to have with him at that time? The only sexually neutral companions allowed seem to be children and perhaps even grandchildren; family still counts, but it is too limited a liberty.

The official nature of sex, or at least its need for official status, is an orthodox, regressive formality. European Union member nations will be required, according to a recent directive, to formally recognize the cohabitation of individuals who, being free to marry or not, decide not to do so. The situation is different for a person who cannot enter into marriage because of previous ties, which sentimentally no longer exist, but which for whatever reason cannot be dissolved, who should therefore be aided in his desire to construct a union corresponding to a marriage that for him is impossible. Apart from these cases, one might ask whether in other situations there is not a contradiction: if two people legitimately feel they do not want to marry or involve the state in the affection and erotic desire that binds them, it is a bit curious if at the same time they demand that the state recognize their bond; it would be like not wanting to subscribe to the theater, which is quite acceptable, yet demand reserved orchestra seats at the performances.

But why shouldn't cohabitation be recognized when two—or why not three or five—people, outside of any sentimental relationship, organize a life together? Or why, in order to be protected—for example, with regard to ownership of a house or recognition of work performed that contributes to day-to-day management—why should they have to declare that they indulge in group sex, perhaps hoping (if that were not to their taste) not to have to demonstrate it before a special investigatory commission? Why should the safeguarding of a person's economic interests, rightly involved in any cohabitation, only be valid in the presence of sexual relations? If there are no children, in which case things would obviously be completely different, and if marriage is rejected on principle, it's unclear why sexual relations should be of greater interest to the general public than those of friendship.

When sex must be made official, socially consecrated and acknowledged, it falls into the conformity typical of radicaloid societies, which aspire to transgression and social consensus at the same time and are an example of perfect philistinism, intolerant in its formal taboos: it is permissible to walk out on your family, but it is not acceptable to leave a dinner after a couple of hours and go to sleep early if you are tired. On the other hand, those couple invitations can also serve as useful signals. A friend of mine, for example, takes advantage of it: when he's invited to a somewhat pretentious dinner for a second time with the same partner, he knows it's time to clear out and break off—or not begin—the so-called relationship.

March 22, 2000

FORGET COLORS

Forget colors? On via Bramante, in Trieste, almost opposite the house where Joyce lived, a sign, printed in block letters with decisive pen strokes, peremptorily urges: "FORGET COLORS!" It is strange to read it on the way back from the sea and the Quarnero (Kvarner) islands, where high summer ignites and by degrees blends all the colors of glory and nostalgia, the honey and gold of the light, the indigo and turquoise of the water, the fleshy pink and red of the oleanders, the black of night, so black as to appear blue. Why forget, instead of holding on to these ageless colors, which for a moment make us feel immortal? Perhaps the unknown author of the sign would say that it is good to forget them for that very reason, because that glimmer of immortality and Eros makes us feel more bitterly the sting of being mortal and knowing that Eros is too, and that white and black are therefore more bearable, more suited to the grayness of life. Or maybe the exhortation to forget tells us that those colors are a lie, a showy picture postcard, a travel agency brochure of fabricated paradises, false promises of true life, a romance novel disguised as a love poem. It may also be that the inscription was written upon awakening from a hallucinogenic state, emerging from visions of tints of unbearable intensity.

Alternatively, perhaps the graffiti is the work of a scientist, cautioning that colors do not exist but are merely light waves that the brain, like a fraudulent simultaneous interpreter, translates improperly into chromatic perceptions. No blue, amaranth, or green, then, but numbers, abstract mathematical signs that measure the wavelengths; so forget colors, as you forget childhood fairy tales later belied by reality. Nevertheless the anonymous author has distinguished colleagues and predecessors: poets, scientists, and philosophers who have discussed colors, from Goethe to Steiner to Wittgenstein. Goethe would certainly take aim at him, as he went after Newton and his formulas, fiercely defending the veracity of the senses and their experience. Red and blue are different wavelengths of light that reach our eyes and our brain, lengths that are numerically quantifiable, but the fact that we see red and blue—and are enchanted by their changing color on an evening—is no less real than those numbers; it is a concrete event of our life and the world. A beloved body is also the sum of countless invisible atoms, but seeing and touching that body is an experience no less objective than the computation of those atoms.

Don't forget colors, then, but remember every nuance, every gleam. Language, unfortunately, is unequal to the variety of their gradations; the DuMont color atlas lists (and reproduces) 999 distinguishable hues, but is forced to name them with number combinations, because no dictionary can be of help. But poetry primarily exists to name things or to create their names; there are perhaps hundreds of writers in the world, each capable of coming up with a name for each of those shades. Who knows, one of them might be the author of that Triestine inscription, who must love colors if he resorted to such harsh rejection; invectives too, as we know, are part of the language of lovers.

September 5, 2000

SACRED AND PROFANE

In a Stockholm bar, toward evening. Outside it is not yet dark: the light lingers on, limpid and poignant, an indefinable nostalgia that seems not to want to fade. There are some Italian students in the bar, mostly Romans; students in their last year of high school, I gather, on some school trip or travel award. Naturally they are looking for Swedish girls. One of them, tall and hefty, more self-assured and exuberant than the others, is holding a young lady on his lap. The reciprocal affectionate caresses gradually become bolder, not at all inhibited by the other young men sitting around them, who every so often interrupt the dialogue, verbal and tactile, between the passionate twosome. At one point the girl, hugging her friend, discovers a medal on his chest, under his shirt; taking it in her hand, she looks at it, points her finger and says, "Maria!" In a flash the young man's hand reemerges from under the girl's skirt and lightly but firmly slaps the feminine fingers holding the image, as he says sternly, "Hey, not so familiar! That's the Madonna!" And so a Catholic education, profoundly steeped in the Marian cult that is notoriously unpopular with Nordic Protestants, reestablishes the distances between the sacred and profane.

November 12, 2000

LOSING YOUR MARBLES

The photograph, which someone sent to the newspaper, is a detail and doesn't do justice to the picture of reality offered by the entire image. Nevertheless, just as a small tissue sample at a histological examination can reveal a person's general condition of health, so maybe a fragment of a page or a chalkboard — like the blackboard in this photo of a classroom at the University of Trieste in which a departmental meeting is taking place — can present the picture of a situation. That vestige covered with numbers, letters, mathematical symbols, arrows, acronyms, circles, parentheses, and erasures is the detail of a portrait, the way the Mona Lisa's lips might be. In this case, it is a detail of a portrait of the Italian university today. These are not calculations bizarrely scribbled by some scientist working on Schrödinger's equation or designing a new type of reactor. They are the figures and operations to which, for months, the professors in every faculty of the Italian university have devoted themselves with mandatory haste, and which have absorbed most of the activities of the academic bodies, departments, curricula, and faculty councils.

They are, that is, the frenetic numerical concoctions aimed at calculating, in obedience to university reforms, how many so-called educational credits must be assigned to a discipline and how many deducted from another, how to divide up the credits to be earned in the two-year specialization and how many to concede to the final exam of one subject or another, all to increase by a handful of small change the funds to be assigned to one or another institution or discipline. There is haggling over how to establish—I quote from a document chosen at random from among countless similar ones—"the percentage of total time reserved for study or other educational activities of an individual type depending on the specific objectives of the advanced discipline and the performance of educational activities of a high experimental and practical content."

Academic meetings turn into agitated lotteries. Crazed maenads of educational credits and fairground hawkers swoop down on the blackboard or feverishly scribble page after page in which they add, subtract, multiply, and divide, parceling out credits to deduct and add, jubilant if they can succeed, by virtue of crafty alliances in the field, in making a dent in the credit assets of a despised colleague. One credit shifted is a euphoric victory, toppling a column of figures that collapses like a wall, leaving the invader an unguarded opening. Battles and tallies continue telephonically at home; hours and hours of congested phone lines in order to form alliances, move didactic capital, adjust curricula, and multiply the special degrees that sprout like mushrooms.

In the meeting room numbers are called out as though people were playing *morra* at the tavern.[3] And as at the tavern, behaviors vary. Some become worked up, shouting and yelling. Some get almost sexually excited. Others are content with the whole brawl because that way there's no time left for the things that should really be done—reading, studying, preparing lessons, and experiments—and any difference between a true scholar and an incompetent is thereby annulled. Oxen would probably be happy to blather at end-less sexology conventions because as long as there's blathering there is no difference between the ox and the bull. There are those who listen with some intimidation, those who don't listen at all, those who don't understand a thing and are content not to understand a thing; some who — though detesting the logorrhea — honestly make an effort to understand and even use the absurdity as best they can in the interest of the students and their studies; others take advantage of the opportunity to do nothing. And some begin to fully com-prehend the meaning of the expression "losing your marbles."

April 1, 2001

A CROWD FOR NO ONE

The snapshot goes back several years and came into my posses-
sion thanks to a colleague of its protagonist, victim or beneficiary
of the episode, who told me about it. An illustrious mathematician
devoted to impervious ultraspecialized studies accessible to only a
few in the field had been invited to teach an annual course at a prestigious interdisciplinary institution, the Collège de France, which
sees the greatest international celebrities of scientific and human-
istic knowledge rotate through its classrooms. The announced
title of the course had already discouraged incompetents, namely,
most of the billions of people on earth, with the exception of a
handful of scattered geniuses, so the scientist, who was expecting
a couple of attendees at most, was astonished to find himself with
an audience of three or four hundred people at the first session.
Obviously he made no concessions to the illustrious audience, not
because he foolishly despised ignorant laymen, like many sacred,
hermetic pseudoaristocrats, often more ignorant than the despised
masses, but simply because his subject did not allow for popular
simplification.

Convinced that it was a mistake, he expected that by the second lecture the crowd would have evaporated. Instead, the crowd
increased at subsequent sessions. At some point, intrigued, he asked
a woman seated in the front row—wearing the look of a typical

assiduous conference attendee—whether the topic and its development were not too difficult, presupposing knowledge that is way too sophisticated, impossible for an average listener. The woman replied seraphically, "Oh, I wouldn't know, we're here because an hour after you Roland Barthes is speaking in this hall; otherwise we won't find a seat."

So the mathematician for the entire year lectured to an overflow crowd that was totally uninterested in him. It seems he didn't mind. Of course, perfection would have been the absolute certainty that in that tarnished audience there was no one, not even one person, who came to hear him; in that way his talk would have achieved an unattainable metaphysical dignity and would have acquired, thanks to that mob of seat seekers, a giddy freedom, a glorious absurdity, the chance to say anything in front of them, even the most senseless and bizarre. Instead the uncertainty of having even a single real listener restricted that freedom, made the huge, intoxicating soap bubble burst, forcing the professor to come down from his illusory cloud, plant his feet on the ground again, be law abiding once more: to give a good lecture, do his job, perform like everyone else his decorous, commendable, and modest role in the theater of the world.

In the end, what happened in that hall is not unlike what more or less happens, albeit in a less evident form, at almost all conferences, in which no one listens to anyone and therefore everyone talks to no one. You take a seat, you put on a serious, nobly interested face the way you put on a tie, and you give yourself up to the drift of your own thoughts, just as the speaker gives himself up to the drift of his own words. So often, and not only in conference halls, we talk without listening to one another and pass each other as distant strangers, promptly swallowed up by the crowd, having left to die the possibility of an encounter, of friendship, of love.

That's not to say that literary figures, such as the one speaking in that hall the following hour, are necessarily more understood than the mathematician when they seduce and titillate their audience. The only difference is that while people realize that they don't understand anything about mathematical formulas—so they at least know that they don't know—they all, or almost all, delude themselves that they understand the writer's metaphors, even convoluted ones, mistaking the vague arousal of the intellectual papillae caused by the images' fireworks for understanding, and therefore they don't even know that they don't know and don't understand. In either case, however, they leave satisfied that they have participated in something important, firmly intending to repeat the experience the following week but glad that for that day it's over. What a relief for everyone, speakers and attendees, when the lecture ends.

February 14, 2002

GROUP PORTRAIT WITH SLEEPING JURIST

The venerable academy, which brings together so many distinguished figures in the arts and sciences, is holding its solemn annual meeting. The president summarizes the year's activities, commemorates the colleagues who passed away, and welcomes the newly elected members; he reads well-wishing messages, announces the upcoming initiatives, takes stock of the financial situation. It is early afternoon, the heavy torpor of the Danubian plains is in the air, and lunch was robust. Beside me, an eminent jurist falls asleep discreetly; the folded arms and reflectively tilted head could also be indicative of absorbed contemplation, and perhaps others, farther away, aren't aware of his slumber. Up close, I see his face slacken, as if the individual parts were relaxing, each on its own, so that it was no longer a face but a random collection of mouth, nose, cheeks, eyelids. The command "break ranks" is still far off; the dress rehearsals, which as the years advance become more frequent for each of us, anticipate it but also exorcise it with decorum.

I look at that face, sleeping, defenseless. Little by little it seems to lose its individuality, its unique traits, and become the face of Everyman, of everyone and no one, generic and expressionless as those of certain neoclassical statues in the parks. I know my sleeping neighbor quite well, his past, his ideas, his passions, and his obsessions; I know what type of women he likes, what he thinks about

God and about the right to strike. At this moment I don't see any of that in his face; sleep has erased it all, the way floodwaters wash away the writings on walls. It has taken away his identity, his consciousness, his beliefs and good manners; it has restored him to dreams, to the unconscious. But it does not seem to have released him from a mask of duties, conventions, censures, imperatives, superstructures which, as we are inclined to think, the conscience or a superego is said to impose and superimpose on the untamed, free truth of the psyche, on the distinct, inimitable uniqueness of desires. By restoring him to the unconscious, sleep seems to have taken away what was most distinctively his; it left him a mask that is virtually interchangeable with that of anyone else. Death and nothingness are the realm of equality, they snuff out differences; perhaps our psyche resembles that indistinct opacity.

Shortly afterward, the time to digest, the cooler air, and the discussions wake my colleague, who, without attracting attention, comes back from the abyss and returns to the rituals and bickering of life, a pallid resurrection. For a few moments around his sunken, sleepy eyes there is that shadow which, in a story by Andreyev,[4] frightened those who met Lazarus risen from the tomb. But he need only rub his eyes, a homespun face-lifting that is more than sufficient, and everything goes back in place, the face is again ready to perform the day-to-day recital. "Sleep and long life" was the well-wishing greeting of the people of Samoa.

March 26, 2002

WE'LL TALK

This year too, as for more than twenty years, we've returned to the small town in the midst of those woods whose fate, for centuries, has been to mark the precarious, persistent boundaries between empires, republics, or realms that history has gradually overthrown without erasing the rifts that divided them. But this time there is only Ida to welcome us for a few days to the inn at the edge of the forest. He, Toni—the husband, innkeeper, proprietor—died a few months ago, though at an age as respectable as that of the trees surrounding the house. Ida welcomes us, shows us to our usual room, tells us about Toni's death and other changes that have occurred in the past twelve months.

After a while, I realize that the conversation is longer than those I've had with her in the past. Indeed, it is the first time she is really speaking with us. The other times she would greet us, prepare the room, and disappear, only to reappear at mealtime, plates in hand. In the meantime she had gathered and cut firewood, swept the floor, washed and ironed the linen, fed the chickens and rabbits, hung the sheets out to dry, and set the table; often she had also gone down to the nearby village to do the shopping. After meals, she cleared the table, said a word or two, and disappeared into the kitchen to wash the dishes. She never told any stories or expressed opinions.

It was he, Toni—whose only task was to pour a glass of wine at the bar now and then to a rare, occasional customer passing through—who talked, spoke his mind, told his stories with spirited, intelligent matter-of-factness. He told us about his military service in the days of fascism, in Abruzzo, about walking back after September 8,[5] about the partisan war in the woods; he commented on local and world politics. In his words were people's destinies and faces, ideas and convictions, images of momentous changes that he had witnessed, passively but aware, for more than three-quarters of a century. I knew what he had done and where he had been, what he thought of politics, the universe, and the Almighty God.

About Ida I knew almost nothing; it had never occurred to her to tell us what she thought about the universe, nor had we thought to ask her. Now, however, all of a sudden, with the death of her husband, Ida had become an individual, a person to talk to, an authority, someone to reckon with. She addressed us with the same familiarity as always, no longer in a few necessary words, but free and talkative. She had lived contentedly with her man, kind and loving to her, but in his shadow. Now that shadow was gone, and she too was visible in the light of day. She was genuinely heartbroken over her Toni's death, but that death had given her an independence and dignity that she had not previously known. Her provincial condition had not offered her the possible recourse often enjoyed by women in a traditional bourgeois marriage (now more or less defunct), the tyranny exacted from a man in day-to-day minutiae, that does not give a woman real autonomy, but rather the demeaning power that servants sometimes have over their masters, while never ceasing to be servants—the man, in this case, remains sultan, though gradually reduced to a eunuch, resigned to consoling himself by gorging on food.

Ida would not even have had the possibility of such retaliations that degrade both the one who resorts to them and the one who is subjected to them. She had not been a master-slave, that is, a harpy; she was simply a slave and therefore retained the obscure dignity of slaves, of subjugation endured out of necessity and without hysteria, of beasts forced to the yoke, and soldiers made to march, indistinguishable from one another yet so much less banal than the officers shouting orders at them. Now Ida has the full dignity of responsibility. It is she who manages the inn and her life; it is she who, like all free men, has things to say. We'll talk, she says, one of these nights we'll talk.

January 26, 2004

THE BANKERS AND THE DEVIL

The snapshot is a television screen, thanks to which I finally understand why so many banks may have been so improvident as to blithely set out to fail. The transmission, in truth, does not dwell on the merits and evils of the banking system but on nonsense such as Satanism and its more or less esoteric cults and followers, rubbish that is not worth speaking about because it belongs to those things that—as a Viennese proverb says—don't even deserve to be ignored, since to ignore them is already too much; it's likely to accord them a disproportionate importance. Mystery—of final things and those of everyday, of the physical and mental universe, of metaphysical questions and the ambiguities of life and of our hearts—has nothing to do with the deceptively hieratic antics of those who make the room so dark that, not seeing anything, one thinks that there is some kind of shadowy ghost hidden there. True religious mystery, says G. K. Chesterton, is found in a clear, sharp light; it can be seen plainly in its complexity.

The alleged initiates of the shadows are either conned or con artists or both. Parapsychologists and occultists who claim to perform miracles through paranormal forces have been careful, for fear of being unmasked, not to accept the challenge of Silvan, the great prestidigitator expertly capable of amazing tricks, who had invited them to perform their magic in his presence. Unfortunately, Silvan did not have the authority of Pope Sixtus V, who, it is said, having an inkling about the superstitious cult of a crucifix that supposedly sweated blood, went before that image, which was no longer properly worshipped but defiled by idolatry, and with great fanfare knelt down and said, "As Christ I adore you," and getting up, added, "and as wood I'll smash you," aiming a nice blow that apparently brought to light a blood-soaked sponge.

On the television show they are talking with insistence—naturally without naming names, esotericism demands secrecy—about high-level bankers who are said to have taken part in satanic rituals, black masses, diabolical liturgies, and so on, perhaps mimicking cults of other societies that make sense in their own context but, recycled elsewhere, are perverted, like certain sacred vessels relegated to knickknacks in the homes of parvenus. Until a couple of nights ago, I thought that bankers dealt with finance; most of them honestly, and some, as happens in the best families, fraudulently. Of course, if they engage in those idiotic devilries instead, it's understandable that the first third-rate fraud who comes along will take them for a ride. If the one responsible for the scams experienced by so many of us is that comic-strip Satan, I'm afraid there is really no hope for us investors, because he doesn't seem to be solvent.

March 1, 2004

ORPHANED EMBRYOS

Of thirty thousand frozen embryos in Italy—Margherita De Bac reports—four hundred "orphans (whose parents cannot be found or that have been disowned) are to be taken to a hospital bank, the IRCCS of Milan's Ospedale Maggiore, and a decision must now be made as to whether and how to use or destroy them."[6] Perhaps the one who decided to separate the fate of the orphans from that of the others is a person who indulges in banal, hyped-up accounts; he may have read, for example, *Freakonomics* by Steven D. Levitt, a puffed-up work that expresses the most conventional, inhumane ideas on these issues. Levitt is a young celebrated economist of the Chicago School, cradle of ultra-anarchist economics. A successful author who, as the flyleaf reports, seduces (or almost) even George W. Bush. In this, as in his previous books, Levitt considers abortion a providential anticrime measure in that it eliminates unwanted children and therefore—in his view—likely future criminals (as if any disadvantage necessarily produced delinquency, as if it were therefore just to eliminate all the disadvantaged, and as if abortions always and solely took place in existentially dramatic situations). If we reason this way, cyclones, earthquakes, and epidemics should also be considered beneficial anticrime measures, especially when they strike Muslim countries, thereby eliminating any number of future Islamic terrorists. Only Flaubert would be able to comment adequately on such reasoning.

Often cruel injustice and inhumanity have a fiercely and bitterly comical aspect, especially when they are cloaked in apparently aseptic, functional rationality. The latter actually proves to be absurdly irrational; a joke, a parody of life and its terms that distorts the human face into a grotesque grimace, into one of those masks that are frightening and at the same time make you laugh. If you believe that scientific research justifies the sacrifice of embryos, like soldiers in battle, why choose those four hundred among the thirty thousand? In the first place, to the great embarrassment of abortionists, embryos are thereby implicitly considered to be human beings, some of whom, since they have no parents, are thought to be destined to a more miserable life and thus more worthy of being eliminated. Based on that criterion, if a crystal gazer were to indicate who among the frozen thirty thousand will be richer tomorrow and who poorer and therefore more prone to adversity, the future underprivileged could be eliminated.

De Bac's report reveals the perversion in which the very just concept of quality of life is often distorted: instead of trying to give a decent quality of life to those who lack it, it eliminates them. Alexander Graham Bell, the inventor of the telephone—according to some, preceded by Antonio Meucci—proposed sterilizing the deaf and dumb, clearly useless to telephony. Aside from the difficulty of establishing what an acceptable quality of life is and who should make that decision, such thinking leads to the horrible, Dostoyevskian vision of a world in which "anything goes" and in which the most monstrous irrationality is disguised as accountable rationality, like a bloodied body concealed by a clean shirt. The orphans of life exposed to this social hygiene are legion; multitudes of suffering, starving, wretched souls of the earth waiting for their hurricane.

January 8, 2006

AN OVERTURNED HEAD OF MEDUSA

In Istanbul, in the northeast corner of the Cistern Basilica, amid the coolness of its mysterious underground water and the symmetry—disquieting, like any symmetry—of its twelve rows of columns in the shadows, two of the columns rest on large Medusa heads, one on its side and one upside down, with their manes of tangled snakes and those eyes that in the myth turn all who gaze at them into stone because they speak of the unbearable, dark horror of existence. When Justinian built the basilica in the sixth century, the marbles of pagan sculptures were evidently used as construction material, perhaps even with the pleasure of humiliating the ancient gods.

But perhaps it is right for a Christian column, with its ascendant impetus, to rest on the infernal Gorgon, the queen of subconscious, shadowy chaos; restrained by the column that dominates her and rises upward, the darkness of the psyche's depths cannot spread and engulf everything like a raging river. It remains contained within its banks, though she continues to support the upward-soaring spirit and, albeit held down and kept in her place, to nourish it with her vital energies, to infuse it with that dynamic drive without which it would be abstract and bloodless, the desert of a self-destructive, false purity, the arid land no longer irrigated by the water of life mentioned in the Apocalypse. It is not surprising that one of the greatest Christian hymns, the "Veni creator spiritus," calls for the senses to be illuminated, not repressed.

That vertical structure is also the layering of civilizations that have followed one another over time, without that succession necessarily implying progress or hierarchical order, but perhaps merely an alternation of worlds and ways of seeing the world, superimposed on one another like strata of earth or fallen leaves, never ultimately disappearing or being superseded. Islamic domes encompass a universe that is not only Turkish or Muslim but also Greek, Latin, Byzantine, Genoese, Venetian, traditionalist, modernist; a crucible and melting pot of cultures, languages, religions. Under there, with her head sideways or inverted, the Medusa, rather than turning you to stone, winks at you.

December 21, 2006

THE SCOURGE OF THE 800 NUMBER

A snapshot, in this case, more sonorous than visual. If the mind were able to be receptive to metaphysical considerations and transcend its own particularity, 800 numbers would not infuriate it, as inevitably happens, but would grant it philosophical serenity. But the heart is small-minded, and the thousands of everyday impediments—leaky dishwashers, plumbers who don't show up, keys that can't be found, noisy neighbors, a new dent on the car, lost cell phones, not to mention cloned credit cards—have a greater effect on one's mood than a morning prayer, a tragic or comforting event in a war zone, the unexpected discovery of a great poem, or an hour of lovemaking, which isn't enough to dispel the grousing that resumes soon after that hour.

For the true philosopher, 800 numbers should be a consolation, because they are one of the few demonstrations that humans are irreplaceable. In fact, the toll-free number, which replaces a human person and should, like a traffic signal, give the green light and allow the goal of the anguished call to be achieved, is a barrier; instead of letting through the unfortunate victim trying to find out how to solve his problem, it forces him into a labyrinth of choices that lead back to themselves and refer him from one blind alley, that is, number, to another, chaining him to the phone like a drowning man clutching a lifesaver heavier than water that drags him down.

Resorting to a toll-free number is often the coup de grâce of rage, which adds to the household drama that made us resort to it and contributes conclusively to the black day that fate has assigned us.

When you enter a phone number, an archaic prejudice imprinted in the genes induces you to expect to talk to someone, with a specimen of your own species, to express your needs to him or her. You don't presume to hear the voice of the telephone operators of the past, young ladies immortalized in a sugary antediluvian film, but a human voice at least. Instead, more and more often you encounter a digital voice, an aseptic, neutral word that does not become flesh and does not reply to your request, but rather subjects you to an arduous choice among various numbers to enter in order to have your cry for help reach someone live. Several numbers, one of which should correspond to your need, but it is often difficult to identify, because life and its snags are wide-ranging and not always clearly reducible to the four or five categories denoted by the numbers to which the inhumane voice on the other end of the line enjoins you to appeal. Moreover, you don't always have the quick reflexes required to assess the range of numbers offered; the voice of the metallic 800 being rattles them off so rapidly that while it is reeling off the services for number 3 you have already forgotten those of number 1.

So you call back, and meanwhile time passes, the urgent problem seems increasingly more pressing; half an hour goes by, an hour, death is a little closer, and the wasted time in which even a small part of your life is consumed is its eloquent precursor. Things get more dramatic when, on top of everything else, it becomes difficult to figure out which of the preestablished categories—listed mechanically on the phone—matches the problem that assails you, and you try frantically to reach a human being, a mortal like yourself, to explain the situation. Reaching a human being is extremely unlikely; when a number, almost always busy, is finally free, the call is automatically forwarded to another metallic voice that reels off other numbers.

And when you finally reach an actual person and explain the pressing problem, the individual, as happens with us mortal humans, is often not able to solve it because the variety and aberrations of life are too complex not only for a machine but also for man, made in its image and likeness. In addition, the rare human interlocutor vanishes quickly into the numbers roulette. All this is nothing compared to what happens, for example, when you lose your baggage at Kennedy Airport in New York; you call the appropriate number, and a recorded voice, speaking fast, tells you to contact such-and-such number if you are arriving from Europe, another number if you are arriving from a U.S. city, and still other numbers depending on the airline with which you've flown, numbers that you don't have time to memorize or jot down before the voice—not a toll-free, but a paid call—hangs up. Humanists can rejoice, even if the lost suitcase counts more than philosophical beliefs, in discovering that the machine has not yet replaced people, in this case a telephone operator in the flesh.

This is not to criticize progress and technology, which greatly alleviate our lives, at least those of us privileged enough to be able to enjoy them; the car, washing machine, or dishwasher liberates existence from much drudgery, making it possible to cultivate the spirit, which would otherwise be overwhelmed and dehumanized by the material effort to survive; they facilitate contacts, relation-ships, acquaintances. All this, provided that elementary good sense use the extraordinary possibilities of technology to simplify life rather than complicate it and increase its difficulties—as do those who take a plane to go from Trieste to Venice, spending ten times as much and taking three times as long compared to the same trip made by train. In reality, the impetus to elude the individual's con-trol—with its power, its need to constantly multiply that power, and its inability to stop—is inevitably intrinsic to technological prog-ress. The 800 number announces an existential revolution, a gen-eral communication that thwarts itself and verges on incommuni-cability. Nevertheless, the problem will resolve itself when on the other end of the line, that of the caller seeking help and advice, there is a digital voice as well, as inhuman and immortal as the one responding to the call.

August 15, 2007

BENEFITS FOR POLYGAMISTS
AND TAXES ON BACHELORS

Photocopy of a newspaper article. In liberal England, a daily reports, family benefits will be granted to Muslim citizens not only for a wife but also for the other women whom the Qur'an permits its followers, who will thereby be able to cultivate their cultural diversity in this respect as well, rightfully so. But perhaps the purse strings should be loosened even further. In Iran, where prostitution is prohibited, there is, to compensate for this onerous proscription, the "fixed-time marriage." It is, in fact, a ritual in which a man and his occasional companion marry before an Islamic cleric, contracting a marriage that is dissolved immediately after its consummation.

But why deprive a woman, a wife for a night (and it not only occurs in Islam), of rights accorded to other wives? It's an offense against the principle of equality. But if it is unfair, in the name of this principle, to discriminate against Muslims, it is equally unfair to discriminate against non-Muslims; the right to have multiple spouses (and therefore collect more family benefits) should therefore be accorded to all — naturally, in our society that has overcome sexist prejudice, to husbands for multiple wives as well as to wives for multiple husbands. But homosexuals have also obtained the right to marry; why discriminate against them, sentence them to settling, unlike the others, for only one spouse? Of course all this should apply not only to marriages but also for couples or polygamous and polyandrous de facto unions. Likewise, one can always hope that Islam too will be open to gender equality and that some day a woman will also be able to have multiple husbands.

Consequently, additional family benefits. Where to find the financial resources for this expense that appears to be growing in geometric proportions? Taxes, obviously. Center-left and center-right, so sensitive to these issues, will therefore presumably have to announce in the next electoral campaign tax hikes for those reasons, certain of finding Italians to be understanding. The burden of those taxes should, in fairness, fall primarily on singles, who enjoy the good fortune of having neither family nor families, of not being overwhelmed by flocks of spouses, former spouses, (ex) in-laws, aunts and uncles and grandchildren of former spouses, and so on. O blessed solitude, o sole beatitude,[7] said the ascetics and hermits; it is just to pay for that privilege. Already fascism, forward-thinking, had taxed bachelors. "Oh my Pippo," says a wife in a poem by Trilussa, after the first night in Naples, "how much better if you had paid the tax on bachelors!"[8]

March 8, 2008

LET THE LITTLE CHILDREN COME UNTO ME

At Vishwanath Temple in Varanasi, dedicated to Shiva, there is a big religious ceremony. It is reached by walking barefoot, as is prescribed, feet sinking into muddy rivulets, through narrow streets guarded by soldiers who stop me because those who are not Hindu are forbidden to enter the temple; however, after my vague statement of being open to a possible conversion, they let me pass. The entrance hall is silent, a monkey leaps among the columns, but inside there is an indescribable throng, repeating invocations to the god, devoutly touching his feet and his huge phallus, tossing flowers into the water, forking out rupees. It is difficult, in that teeming mass, to think about the Rigveda, the Upanishads or the Bhagavad Gita, about the texts of Indian mysticism — one of the greatest such doctrines of all time — that Biagio Marin used to read aloud to me beside his sea at Grado. But then again, the request to extract the heart from the body of John Paul II, recently advanced by a high-ranking Polish prelate, is also quite far removed from evangelical simplicity.

Here Brahma, the One, shows his face of Shiva, the multiform god of sex and destruction, who, as in the marvelous caves on Elephanta Island in Mumbai harbor, displays an unsettling serenity. The countless gods and their innumerable forms are the infinite, changing faces of life, of its multiplicity that is not dissolved in the

One; if to our eyes the ceremony seems like an irreverent carnival, maybe it is because every representation of the unrepresentable Absolute is always fraudulent desecration, suited to our increasingly profane existence. Of course, in Sarnath, the town about six miles away where Buddha is said to have preached the Sermon of Benares on pain and suffering, the feeling is very different. There—or at the place to which this refers—something fundamental happened in the history of the world, as in Christ's Sermon on the Mount; something that affects everyone, for all time.

When I leave the Temple of Shiva, the hordes on the street are no less dense. Swarms of beggars; the embarrassment that every beggar—genuine, false, tragic actor, or ham, intrusive but, as Pirandello said, never dull—produces in the flustered visiting foreigner. Children beg as soon as they can stand up, along with old people, the maimed, and the crippled, who arouse pity and suspicions of horrific mutilations. A beautiful young woman with a baby at her breast, her legs and slim bare feet the color of mud, meets my eye for a moment, like one of the *passantes* in the instant complicity that Brassens sang about,[9] and I realize, by the triumphant expression in her eyes, that she knows, for sure, that I will give her the donation she asks me for.

Shortly afterward, a little girl with an infant in her arms begs for alms. Her face is very pure, with the smiling, gentle grace of childhood, and she easily inspires a protective tenderness and a desire to give. Behind her, unseen by her, an elderly cripple approaches unsteadily, hand outstretched toward me. When the child notices him, her face hardens, her eyes narrow maliciously, she shouts something at him and shoves him away with a kick, knocking him to the ground. The old man gets up and walks away hobbling, cross-ing the street all bandy-legged. The little girl, with the baby in her arms, moves off to another car stopped at the traffic signal. Yet Jesus said, "Let the little children come unto me, for the kingdom of God is for those like them . . ."

July 6, 2008

PISSING AGAINST THE WIND
AND *CONTRA LEGEM*

Trieste's municipal councillor in charge of Public Works, Franco Bandelli, denounced, with the approval of many citizens, the habit—evidently increasingly widespread in my city—of peeing in the street, a trend that leads "ill-mannered young men from good families to go and piss on walls, doors, and parked cars." It is not so much the result of the gradual disappearance of the old, glorious *vespasiani* (public urinals), swept away by restorations and public works projects, as of a number of different factors: the increasing consumption of beer, a lesser moral sensitivity toward outdoor urination (no longer viewed as transgressive, similar to other habits once socially reproached and now socially acceptable), and an insufficient number of law enforcement officers (especially municipal police) assigned to deter the offense or to impose the fines recently enacted by the city of Trieste for those who pee on a public street. Truthfully, I hadn't noticed the spread of the phenomenon, and I don't see much evidence of it in the streets, but clearly that must be due to my distraction or perhaps to the culpable egoism of a man of letters, insensitive to the needs—in a literal and figurative sense—of the community.

Of the three main causes of the deplorable practice, the decline of the vespasiano is perhaps the most significant. The problem, however, is not just limited to Trieste, despite the fact that Trieste, a key Mitteleuropean city yet still provincial, is now belatedly facing an emergency that had already struck Milan in 1981, an emergency described with hilarious humor and unbridled linguistic fantasy by Alberto Cavallari in his masterful kaleidoscope *Vicino & Lontano* (Near and Far). With the disappearance or ever rarer availability of "the old green temple"—albeit deplorably sexist, since it offered relief only to a man standing up—the Milanese authorities at the time, besieged like a medieval castle with a moat increasingly full of sewage and desperately searching for solutions, at some point thought of acquiring the brand-new electronic toilets that Jacques Chirac, then mayor of the Ville Lumière, had installed in Paris. Maybe—Cavallari insinuated—because they were obsessed with envy for the much acclaimed modernity or postmodernity of the Beaubourg. The desire for technological innovation was and is still alive even in Trieste; years ago, in fact, the municipal councillor Paolo Rovis had already proposed installing several UriLifts, the re-tractable cylindrical urinal.

It is not however surprising that Milan gave up the Parisian idea, perhaps fearing that in case of malfunction the automatic operation of the French vespasiano, which released a purifying whirlwind of water and detergents, might let loose too soon and drench the user. If such glitches were to occur frequently, they would stir protests and disturb the social peace. The second factor, beer, has a weighty impact; not only due to a purely physiological process, common to any liquid, but because of the relationship, in this case privileged, between the input and output of the liquid, attested to by the English gentleman who wondered thoughtfully whether the pleasure of drinking the beer was more intense or that of expelling it shortly afterward was. But the authorities in a liberal country, moreover one increasingly pervaded by radical ideologies adverse to any prohibition, can't do anything about the consumption of beer except as regards minors.

What remains crucial is the intervention of the forces of law and order, which, as we know, can't materially prevent crimes but can discourage them with their sanctions. But that's where apprehension arises, because the municipal police force does not have enough staff, it is already difficult to patrol the streets, the unions are opposed to extending the duties and "increasing the officers' duty shifts for anti-pee rounds," there are no funds for overtime, after two a.m. the cops no longer work, and the job would therefore fall to the flying squad and the carabinieri, who may have good reason to believe their role is to prevent worse crimes.

Trieste, moreover, has an additional problem with respect to Milan: the sea, the place par excellence where urinating is tacitly accepted, though no less inappropriate since it represents a desecration of that setting and element of the world that more than any other evokes the infinite, Eros, the divine. According to an old Portuguese tradition, pissing in the sea is a sin, albeit venial. But how to apprehend the offenders? In eighteenth-century London it was forbidden to pee in the Thames, and sentinels stationed on its banks could easily catch the culprits in the act, just as guardians of the law, unconcerned about being splashed, could have done in my high school days, when Trieste's wintry sea, whipped up by the bora, covered Molo Audace and froze over; it was a manly ritual to go to the end of the pier, braving the slippery ice and the danger of ending up in the waves, and urinate in the sea without worrying about the direction of the wind.

But how can you catch them when they do it in the sea, standing underwater? Employ scuba divers, frogmen, deep-sea divers? The volunteer patrols hoped for by the Northern League to keep watch on immigrants would surely be willing to make up for the shortage of police in the "anti-pee rounds," but their places of origin, usually from the plains or mountainous lands, make them unsuitable for underwater operations. Lenin's big question is still current: What is to be done?[10]

August 31, 2008

THE MENU OF THE REVOLUTION

A menu—a good menu—is a comforting image of what lies ahead. All the more so if a nobility of spirit is combined with the pleasures of the flesh, a spirit ready for anything, as Scripture says, even for revolutions and not just at the table. "*Harco* (a spicy soup of the Caucasus) is typically made with beef brisket, but a substitute for the latter can also be mutton brisket. . . . An hour, an hour and a half, after it begins to boil, add the minced onion, crushed garlic, rice, sour plums, salt and pepper and cook for another 30 minutes. Stew the tomatoes slightly in butter . . ."

This and other mouth-watering recipes, from plov or pilaf of Uzbekistan to Ukrainian blini, are not found in just any collection, but appear in a "revolutionary" text, namely *The Book of Tasty and Healthy Food*, first published in Moscow in 1939 and reprinted, with rich illustrations, several times over the years by the Soviet Union's Academy of Medical Sciences. The book, at Stalin's express wish, was to attest to the "Revolution in the kitchen" and document "the greatest affirmation of the steady progress of society's material and cultural needs" promoted by the Communist Party, crowning "the felicitous realization of quinquennial plans" with the "health, happiness and joy of living" attained by workers, and women in particular.

A precious book for us, who can afford to put the result of those succulent recipes on our plates, *The Book of Tasty and Healthy Food*, now translated and interpreted by Ljiljana Avirović against the terrible Soviet history of those years, was nevertheless a tragic joke for millions of starving, undernourished Soviet citizens of that time. Scientists and intellectuals of various disciplines collaborated on the recipe book; "the engineer of souls"—that is, the writer and intellectual who according to Stalin must produce the new man of Communist society—does not overlook the table, where not only the body is regenerated but also the spirit, the cordial sense of living. "A man is reborn by living life to the fullest": Stalin said that, toasting generously at a sumptuous dinner on October 26, 1932, at Gorky's home, in front of literati and writers whom Gorky was assigned to train, educate, shape, and regiment according to the directives of the supreme leader, who that evening is a jovial epicure, satisfied to see that regime's factory of intellectuals is operating as it should. Good meals have always helped the masters and their chosen favorites to dominate those with empty stomachs.

At that excellent dinner, in fact, plans are made for a collective educational trip for 120 writers chosen by Gorky to travel, in four train cars of the special Red Arrow, to visit the Gulag, the prisons of "reeducation through physical labor" scattered along the Bjelomor Canal, built with the appalling, frightful forced labor of prisoners and their mass slaughter. *Bjelomor*, the book jointly written by thirty-six authors under Gorky's guidance, was released in 1934. This apologia of slavery includes a prisoner's daily menu, which to Ljiljana Avirović seems unlikely: "Half a liter of fresh cabbage soup, 300 grams of polenta with meat, 75 grams of fish cutlets with sauce, 100 grams of phyllo pastry with white cabbage."[11] By contrast, food and menus are fully present in these writers on a school trip; Saša Avdeenko, a young man with a hearty appetite, writes, "We ate and drank what we wanted and as much as we could: smoked sausages, cheeses, caviar, fruit, chocolate, wine, cognac, without paying anything."

That cookbook is a marginal footnote on the page of the Soviet Union's history and the tragic perversion or failure of its proclaimed values. To think of the table, where food and wine can become not only a form of nutrition but a form of family communion and friendship, is a true revolutionary thought, which envisions a liberated life, lived happily in spite of time passing. Perhaps Lenin was thinking of this when he said that a good homemaker could be a commissar of the people, because those feminine virtues, freed from oppression, are indeed the art of living and political wisdom. There is a profound nobility in the plan to liberate woman, through the proper organization of work, from the domestic labors that oppress her, allowing her to be a mother who provides food and love but is free to pursue other interests, as men are. The Revolution, in theory, does not aim to deprive the evangelical Martha of the love that drives her to the stove, but would afford her the chance to not be crushed by that work and to listen, like Mary, to the Word.

Brutally contradicted by Soviet reality, this vision contains within it a genuine, though in this case merely utopian, ideal of redemption. It is true that man is "reborn by living life to the fullest" and all the better when accompanied by a good glass of cognac; the tragedy is that the individual speaking those words, that evening in October 1932 in front of a table of slaves disguised as engineers of souls, is Comrade Stalin, who is oppressing, starving, and

exterminating millions of men. Even in difficult times the powerful eat well. *The Book of Tasty and Healthy Food* also includes the
menu offered by Stalin on September 21, 1944, to Tito—"a giant
and a dandy," the journalist Enzo Bettiza once described him. The
dinner served to Tito by Stalin included red caviar, marinated sturgeon and eel, lightly pickled cucumbers, Georgian goulash in wine
with gnocchi, Russian-style chicken on the spit, jarred mushrooms,
fritters, and blueberries.

Bread and wine, which on a table fraternally laid are a seal of
humanity, become obscene debauchery in the orgy of the powerful
who divide up the cake and delude themselves that they are divid-
ing up the world, as when Churchill and Stalin in Moscow split a
superb sturgeon and divided up the unfortunate Balkan nations, 75
percent of Romania for the Soviets and 25 percent for the English,
the opposite for Greece, and so on; meanwhile Churchill, slicing
himself a choice morsel, ceded territories not knowing, he would
confess, exactly where they were, such as Bessarabia. Ten years later,
in the 1954 edition, the collective introduction to *The Book of Tasty
and Healthy Food* states that, for the good of the country, it is "necessary to introduce tomato juice as a drink for the masses."

May 4, 2009

ON THE ROCKY BEACH

On the riviera of Barcola, in Trieste. Riviera, so to speak; a thin strip of rocky coastline, a free beach that runs along the main road to the city, water that quickly becomes deep, tamarisks on the shore, foamy as waves, a vast, open expanse of sea, which in childhood gave a sense of oceanic immensity, in a sentimental education in which the bond between Fray and the sea was learned for all time. The people in bathing suits, not at a lido resort or on a real beach but just outside the city, practically already in the city, give the impression of being committed to and enjoying life.

Trieste is not only a crossroads between East and West, as its legend states, but also one between North and South, between Scandinavian melancholy of certain winter sunsets and the southern vitality of summer. Beyond the gulf, where Italian waters become Slovenian and then Croatian, you can see the cathedral of Pirano, the centuries-old footprint of Saint Mark's lion in Istria, and farther on Punta Salvore, with its lighthouse and pine trees in the wind. The population that every day from May to October comes to the rocky strip in Barcola is set in its ways; by tacit convention, each of us has his place on the beach, generally respected by his neighbors, with whom polite relations are maintained but without getting too familiar. Every so often the threat of bans, announced in the newspapers, hovers—the menace of regulatory plans, of the construction of fee-based facilities or touristy marinas—which so far have been thwarted each time by truculent letters to the editor and the authorities from men who wield the pen, numerous and assiduous among the swimmers, as well as by protests from Triestines who for years have resided in New York or Adelaide but haven't forgotten that rocky shore. The authorities, in truth, seem to understand that *tocio,* the freedom to have fun or take a little dip, is a public good, a beneficial quality of community life, and they worry about free showers and the tamarisks.

A few years ago the beach had risen to prominence in the news thanks to a drowning in which the body, brought back to shore and covered with a sheet, had been left for a long time in the midst of beachgoers, who went on sunbathing, unperturbed, beside it, in that easy indifference of life toward death that the intense, scorching summer light renders even more ruthless. The cloth that covered the man seemed not so much a sign of respect for him and for the inviolable universal mystery that had happened to him and in which he had entered, as of regard for the bathers, so that they would not be disturbed by death's intolerability and effrontery. Only a child stared curiously at that shape on the ground, perhaps without really understanding what had happened, the way a dog sniffs at something unfamiliar to him.

Few disruptions, rare disturbances to the public peace. A mother scolds her son, a boy of four or five playing with a delightful little girl his same age—black as ebony, evidently adopted by her parents, two Germans who have settled a little farther away—shooting a water pistol and leaping over the bodies stretched out in the sun, for him not yet desirable or provocative. Reprimanded, the boy protests, saying that then the girl should be scolded as well. "What girl?" the mother asks, not seeing the child who is hiding behind a tree. "The one who talks funny so you can't understand a word," he says, clearly struck by the fact that the little girl uses words that for him are incomprehensible and a little miffed to discover that things can have other names.

It doesn't occur to him to identify her by the color of her skin, though it stands out noticeably even among the suntanned bathers; the difference in color, which in other situations could have caused, and perhaps may still cause, separation and segregation, is irrelevant compared to the difference between his Italian and her German. Not even that, however, has the power to separate them, because, as soon as the girl reappears, having been duly admonished (in German) by her parents in the meantime, the two quickly resume their chasing and squirting, unaware that they have had a nice lesson on diversity and identity, themes that, for that matter, are also dear to the cultural-bathing conferences so frequent on summer beaches—at least those resorts that are somewhat more elegant than the rocky strip in Barcola.

August 10, 2009

A NEW WRITER

The Censor

I learn belatedly, thanks to the seaside indolence of August on a Dalmatian island that piles up stacks of outdated newspapers and weeklies, that in Denmark they have purged—I imagine from the schools—a tale by Hans Christian Andersen with a Christian ending, or Christian elements in any case, so as not to offend the faithful of other churches. In its respectful stupidity, this is a decisive step in the universal history of censorship. In this case, it is a well-intentioned censorship, moved by a concern not to upset cultural or religious minorities. But censorship, after all, is always well-intentioned: it seeks to protect morality, one's country, the family, institutions, order, society, progress, the people, the children, health. In this case, a new formula is chosen: instead of burning a book or forbidding followers to read it, as did the *Index librorum prohibitorum* at one time,[12] the book is adapted to the alleged needs of the readers, a little like the adaptations of literary masterpieces for children that were used in the days of my childhood, or scholastic editions of the classics, in which the risqué passages—for example, in the *Odyssey*, Odysseus shipwrecked on the island of the Phoenicians who comes out of the sea naked—were replaced by a series of suspension points.

In the nineteenth century a Barnabite or Piarist priest, worried that the suspension points might cause the kids' imaginations to gallop dangerously, substituted verses written by himself, decorously innocuous, in the masterpieces he had to explain to his pupils, so that Andromeda's bare breasts became waves crashing on the rocks, and so on. If this grotesque example were followed, it would involve a huge increase in jobs, as would, for instance, the proposal for high school instructors to teach in dialect. Hundreds, thousands of texts to purge, abridge, expand, correct, rewrite. In a democratic country, censorship is the same for everyone; repressive tolerance—or repression in the name of tolerance—is the salt of democracy. According to these paradoxical criteria, Alessandro Manzoni should be entirely stripped of his Catholicism and his faith in Providence, any trace of Epicurean materialism should disappear from Lucretius, and every Leopardian meaning of life from Giacomo Leopardi, not to irritate anyone. In fortunate epochs of anticommunism like ours, Bertolt Brecht should be radically divested of every Marxist or otherwise revolutionary nuance, while Rudyard Kipling, on the other hand, should be relieved of his British imperialist ideas, albeit happily contradicted by his imaginative sensibility, not to offend the Indians.

Based on this aberrant though rigid logic, censorship should be especially pitiless toward religious texts, particularly objectionable to those who do not share their beliefs. The Qur'an is fine as long as all references to Allah and His Prophet are removed. The Gospel, too, contains many subversive things that displease Catholics, Protestants, the Orthodox, Muslims, and atheists; Jesus who lashes the merchants, drags the apostles away from their families and even questions the bond between himself and his mother,[13] bothers many people. Not to mention when he says that to save one's life one must lose it, or forbids worrying about tomorrow and praises the lilies of the field that neither reap nor work but are worth more than the glory of Solomon; for ultra-capitalists of the Chicago School it is an intolerable blasphemy that must be purged.

But censoring Dante or Manzoni out of regard for non-Catholics would not be enough. Even among the latter there are not only saints like Fra Cristoforo, but also many cowardly Don Abbondios, many mellifluous prelates similar to the Father Provincial who out of political expediency bends to the arrogance of the count, his uncle, and many women like Donna Prassede convinced that they are interpreting to perfection God's will that they identify with their own. For severely bigoted and reactionary Catholics there should be editions of Manzoni's *Promessi sposi* (The Betrothed) adapted to their tastes; editions, for example, in which Cardinal Federigo praises Don Abbondio for his conformism and turns a blind eye to the cravings of Don Rodrigo, who is more worthy of note than two poor devils like Renzo and Lucia. For traditionalists, all Greek poetry should be cleansed of every homosexual reference; for others, instead, all stories in which the lovers are heterosexual should be banned in erotic novels, insofar as they are an implicit though tacit offense to those who are not.

All in all those editors who impose—often, it seems, in the United States—a happy ending on a novel that the author had concluded in tragedy or vice versa, according to their reckoning of the audience of the moment, are indeed doing something similar. Such revisions would create work for legions of unemployed writers. Literary history would even be enriched by all these variants; every artist transformed into Proteus, every book personalized and tailor-made for the potential reader, a Library of Babel that has been further multiplied. Everyone would be content, since his expectations and demands would be met and his convictions never challenged. A book, said Paul Valéry, helps us not to think, and that is what, deep in our hearts, each of us wants most fervently.

August 30, 2009

THE WALL WILL LAST FOR YEARS . . .

Recollection of a day in Blois, France, the first week of November 1989, on the occasion of a conference organized by Jack Lang on the subject of Eastern Europe, or what used to be called "the other Europe," a term that indicated the fact that those countries were members of the Soviet bloc yet that also expressed a disdainful condescension, a deep-seated prejudice toward the East, a kind of second-class Europe. As our quiet, innocuous discussions unfold, the big protest in East Berlin is exploding in all its intensity, and of course immediately becomes the center of all the debates, opinions, expectations, hopes, fears, and predictions. A young film director from East Berlin, actively involved in the protest, shows up unexpectedly. During the few hours he spends with us, to return as soon as possible to resume his place in the struggle in Berlin, he relays excitedly what is going on in the city's streets, down to the smallest detail of that wave that is engulfing the entire world, much more than we realize at the moment. Shortly before leaving, he says that any prediction about the course of events is impossible, that nothing can be ruled out, not even a bloody repression; only one thing is certain, he says emphatically: the Wall will unfortunately last for years yet. Two or three days later, the Wall was down; it had been reduced to a few broken-down ruins, an old piece of junk from the past, and he was one of those who had actively played a part in knocking it down.

He could not imagine that the Wall would fall, just as none of us could imagine it or think it possible, convinced, like him, that the Wall would last for who knows how long. We are almost all blind curators, reluctant or otherwise unable to believe that things can change. We mistake the reality in which we are used to living for nature, for an order of things that it would perhaps be desirable but ingenuous to hope to change. We mistake the facade of what's real for the only possible, definitive reality, without noticing what is constantly, incessantly pressing behind it and continually changing it—at times slowly, almost inadvertently, at other times at a sensational pace.

We don't hear the worm gnawing the wood, we don't notice the chrysalis that will become the butterfly, we don't perceive the clogging of History's arteries. Anyone who, in October of '89, had said that the Berlin Wall would collapse very soon, and that in place of fallen ideological walls other ethnic and social walls—harsh suppressions, narrow-minded, oppressive micro-nationalisms—would rise, would have been considered a hothead.

A year later, on October 3, 1990, I attend the celebration for the reunification of Germany. In the window of a store numerous television sets show what is happening in the various zones of Berlin. On one screen, at a certain point, Günter Grass can be seen speaking, contentious and torrential; the mouth opens aggressively under the showy mustache, but no sound comes from the other side of the glass, as in a silent film.

November 5, 2009

LIMPING VERSES FROM THE HEREAFTER

Sisi is back, with the face of Cristiana Capotondi, in the television miniseries directed by Xaver Schwarzenberger. There are many Sisis: the captivating, melancholy woman, fragile yet unmovable in her loyalty to her demons; the restless empress, rebelling against court etiquette and intolerant of duties connected to her role though freely accepted; the nostalgic traveler of distant lands; the health fanatic obsessed with caring for her body and working out; the urbane sophisticate who introduces the first bathtub in the royal palace; the anorexic; the tragic, random sacrificial victim of a senseless crime. There is also the poet, author of many delicate, unconvincing, limping verses that she maintained had been dictated to her from the hereafter by Heinrich Heine through a medium she used. At which an inspired court counsellor, who has unfortunately remained anonymous, quipped, "It appears that Heine, after he died, took a turn for the worse."

March 1, 2010

THE STRAY AND A MODEL

This time the snapshot is not metaphoric, but real, a photograph taken in Moscow, in front of the Mendeleyevskaya metro station, published in the *Financial Times* and other world newspapers. It is a statue, in bronze, of a small-to-medium-size stray dog; an indeterminate breeding mixture generated a short, dark-grayish coat with lighter tones here and there, and a head that is a cross between a fox and a sled dog. The face that looks up at you in the statue, waiting for food or to welcome you warmly, required millions and millions of years of evolution in the world, odysseys of neurons; yet he exited the scene—at least as Malchik, that was his name—in a few seconds on a winter evening

On that evening Yulia Romanova, a twenty-two-year-old model, was walking through that crowded Moscow metro station with her little dog, a Staffordshire terrier whom she had just taken to a tailor who specialized in designing the latest style apparel for dogs, such as the terrier's elegant green coat she'd just bought. One can surmise that the terrier's mistress, like many models and showgirls, had managed to ruin the seductive sacredness of carnal beauty— which, free of icy or garish poses, is a salt of the earth—by rendering it aseptic and neutral. Malchik had made his home in a corner of the station; he was known to the many people who streamed by there each day like a flood, and in fact had a name, which is uncommon for a stray dog, especially in a city like Moscow, where there are thirty-five thousand of them.

When the model and her terrier approached, Malchik, accustomed to defending his spot, barked at them, a bark and nothing more, at which Miss Romanova, quick as a flash, pulled a kitchen knife out of her pink handbag—an unusual object among the lipsticks and eyeliner pencils—and stabbed him to death. Arrested, she was sentenced to a year of psychiatric treatment, perhaps understandable in her case, but always worrying in a former Soviet country. The gratuitous stabbing that slaughtered Malchik is a small slash on the face of God, certainly a paltry scratch compared to the appalling atrocities that constantly disfigure Him. Still, Malchik is missed by his random, hurried metro friends, who wanted to remember him by erecting that statue. It is unlikely that anyone will want to dedicate a statue to Yulia Romanova when her time comes.

March 31, 2010

AT THE SEASHORE

The *scogliera*, or rocky strip—that's what Triestines call Barcola's narrow beach that runs along the road and skirts the sea, where many like to swim in the deep, open waters that evoke oceanic vastness and make you forget you're at the end of the small Adriatic. Among the fairly numerous group of people lying on the side of the road in bathing suits is a couple somewhere between so-called middle age and something more, years that have been used but are worn well. The woman is rather pretty, a curvy femininity, happily and moderately plump, that combats the wrinkles of time; only the mouth has something hard about it, the coldness that mindfulness of one's social class and a defensive mechanism will sometimes stamp on reserved lips. The man is sitting, looking blankly and glumly at the sea and fiddling with a cap, a needless defense against the sun in the declining days of summer.

A little farther on there is another couple, much younger, with a little girl, obviously troubled and unpredictably unsettled in her outbursts and unmotivated mood swings. She has beautiful dark eyes and a captivating smile, often distorted into an uncontrollable scowl that accompanies some sudden aggressive act, spitting on the ground or uttering a vulgar word, so sadly jarring on a mouth that has all the grace of childhood. Curiosity about her soon turns to annoyance when she throws herself on the ground, beating her feet repeatedly on the rocks. As enigmatic silent tears roll down her cheeks, she suddenly notices the cap the man is twirling in his hands and smiles, watching him intently. The man returns her gaze and her smile and abruptly throws her his cap. The child catches it, laughs as though complicit, shows it triumphantly to the neighbors, then goes over to him, rubs it on his face and puts it on his head. After a while she wanders away, suddenly clouded over. The man's wife—the wedding band on her ring finger sanctions such a conjecture—turns to him, irritated, her voice as hard as her lips: "You know you shouldn't do that to me. I'm too sensitive, it hurts me to see a little girl that way; I already have my own sorrows and I don't need to see more of them."

Rarely does brutality have the intelligence and honesty to declare itself; sensitivity is the best disguise for egoism, its most effective advocate because it is convinced of what it is saying, even if it is false. Everyone is anguished and sensitive; we all are, so sensitive to the pain of others that we shove it aside so it won't ruin our appetite. There are people, Georges Bernanos wrote, so sensitive that they can't even stand to see an insect suffer; they crush it immediately so as not to watch it suffer anymore. Meanwhile, the presumed husband, not knowing what to say or what to do, puts the cap back on his head.

September 25, 2010

THE PLACE WHERE THE HEART IS SILENT

Her name, the caption says, is Koo-tuck-tuck. Once again the snapshot is not a metaphor but a real photograph, taken by Geraldine Moodie at Cape Fullerton, Hudson Bay, in 1905. She is a young Eskimo woman, or rather Inuit, as one must say today to be politically correct, because Inuit, meaning "person" or "people," is what they call themselves, feeling somewhat offended by the term "Eskimo," given to them by the Algonquin Indians and picked up by the early European travelers, which means "raw-meat eaters." Koo-tuck-tuck is photographed against a dark background, wearing pants and a fur jacket adorned with vivid geometric patterns; the black and white image lets you merely imagine the colors, probably those of flowers during the tundra's brief summer. Under the thick, soft, plump clothing a graceful, almost slender body can be divined, unusual among her people, the airy feminine gentleness of a birch. But it's the face that is unforgettable. A perfect oval, pale under the long, sleek black hair; a look of unspeakable and proud sadness, utterly free of the complicit yet hostile submission so frequently found in false—and even real—indigent peoples and among marginalized social or ethnic groups.

Other Inuits photographed by Geraldine Moodie pose nicely; they know that their harpoons and their kayaks are a big hit in the great world that they know little about but whose game they have instinctively understood; they enjoy performing the role of the Inuit while trying to earn a little money. She-nuck-shoo, mustached like the walruses he hunts, with a sharp, intelligent look acts like any of us, playing the part of himself—a salutary game that prevents looking deeply into the unbearable darkness of life, our own and that of others. If we were truthfully and openly ourselves, without pressure suits or scripts to recite, we would probably be lost, exiles from who knows where, seeking political asylum in a madhouse.

Koo-tuck-tuck's black eyes, above the perfect nose and gentle, serious mouth, look directly into that darkness, staring into a void with no railings. In that look there is only life, naked, wounded, and inexplicable. Koo-tuck-tuck, the caption says, is deaf and mute. It is not difficult to imagine what such a disability might have meant, especially at that time, particularly deafness, in a world in which the slightest whisper can be a final message, the creaking that warns of a crack in the ice and the opening of a chasm, the presence of a beast from whom to flee or one you mustn't let get away if you want to survive. The Inuit of Canada—who now have an autonomous region, Nonavut, and self-government—speak Inuktitut, whereas in Greenland there was a more articulate cultural tradition more open to writing. In the region where Koo-tuck-tuck lived the Reverend Edmund Peck had only recently arrived to teach his people to transcribe their language—that is, to read and write—and it is unlikely that she would have been able to communicate through writing or that the Inuits would have been familiar with real sign language.

Excluded from the oral culture that constitutes the soul of her people, Koo-tuck-tuck, perhaps, can only watch. A gaze into the absolute void of the ice fields, of the silence that surrounds her—

there is a bay that, in the language of the Inuit, is called "the place where the heart is silent"—and into the inexpressibility of her existence. How does Koo-tuck-tuck live, what does she desire, how does she love, alone with that gaze, perhaps abandoned to her incommunicability? Under the deafening roar of history is the silence of the last and the forgotten, to whom speech was never granted but who perhaps for this very reason are the persons most made in the likeness of God, of whom the Song of Moses asks: "Who is like You among the mute?" And perhaps Koo-tuck-tuck is one of those stones rejected by the builders, which Scripture says the Lord made the cornerstone of His house. Her unreachable, reserved beauty speaks of a solitude greater than that of the Arctic; perhaps a solitude similar to love if it is true, as Charles Louis Philippe wrote, that "love is everything that you don't have."

November 19, 2010

ON THE TRACKS

A December evening. Snow and bad weather have paralyzed airports, stations, and highways, causing huge, nerve-racking delays. In Milan's busy station a Eurostar would be ready to depart, but it has been chaotically stormed by passengers disgorged by other stranded trains, left high and dry by missed connections, who now, squeezed together and standing, crowd into the train tagged for passengers with a valid ticket and reservation, who are sitting, impatiently, in their rightful seats, all of which are occupied. Railway employees urge the squatters to get off so that the train—which according to regulations cannot be given the green light when it's overloaded like that—can finally start moving. None of the unauthorized occupiers moves; each of them, in a mutual and suspicious general solidarity, waits for someone else to make a move, while the conductors keep pressing, more and more futilely and fretfully authoritative. The ticketed passengers sitting comfortably in their seats glare sullenly at those crammed together, standing; there are protests, strong words are hurled, the more legalistic among the transgressors call for an exception to the rules given the exceptional circumstances.

In the horde of squatters is an unfortunate man who, squashed against the train door, evidently piled in last; ordered to get off ever more imperatively by a railway man on the platform in front of him, he is berated by a corpulent wife, in turn crushed against him, admonishing him not to be the usual fool incapable of asserting himself and ready to give in. The railway man with the martial cap—his co-workers have gone off somewhere—takes it out on him since he's the one he finds himself face to face with. The poor wayfarer, caught between the fire and the frying pan, doesn't know which way to turn. He feels alone before the Law, ready to make him the scapegoat, but whereas breaching the Railway's rules involves a brief hassle, his wife's vituperation is a life sentence. The more imperious the train conductor becomes, revealing the bossy vocation latent in every male, the more the wife wrings and twists the man like a piece of laundry. He doesn't answer either one; he tries to look elsewhere, toward an empty spot.

In the vestibule of the train car an ancient rite of retaliation unfolds: woman's revenge against centuries of male abuse of power; against explicit or implicit violence, arrogance, exclusion repaid by daily domestic tyranny, which while granting the man the official crown as head of the family, robs him of material freedom, routines, and desires. A war between mice and frogs—*batrachomyomachia* it was called in Homer's time—in which everyone loses; the slave who enslaves his master, wrote Simone de Beauvoir, does not thereby become free. A war that is perhaps drawing, laboriously, to an end; there is progress after all. At a certain point the man, under pressure from the Law, gets off, followed by his infuriated wife, who is immediately rewarded by the satisfaction of having been right, because as soon as he gives in, the only one of the squatters to do so, the train departs in spite of the regulations, leaving him alone on the platform at the mercy of his maenad; both grow smaller and smaller to those observing them from the train as it moves away, no longer able to hear them but able to guess what they are saying, watching the contrite face of the one and the incensed face of the other vanish.

January 31, 2011

THE SACRED HOURS

In this case it is not a photograph, but the photocopy of a page or some of its lines. In his book *Nobility of Spirit: A Forgotten Ideal*, Rob Riemen recalls how Thomas Mann's wife and daughter, when the radio broadcast the news of the outbreak of World War II on September 1, 1939, hesitated to inform him so as not to disturb the "sacred hours" when he attended to his literary creation. It is hard to imagine an offense against humanity as equally barbaric and absurd as those respectful huddles about whether to knock on the great writer's door, whether to interrupt those "sacred hours," while one of the most appalling tragedies of history was unfolding. The writer—and with him his wife and daughter—knew very well what was at stake; Mann had already grasped and denounced the infamy of Nazism, he had left Germany for that reason, he is the representative par excellence of democracy, of humanism, of humanity threatened by the most atrocious violence. Even if the fury that a few years later would become Auschwitz was inconceivable in 1939, the racist, murderous rage of the Third Reich was very clear, to Mann in particular.

Mann is a great writer to whom much is owed, but at that moment—his fault? that of the women in his family?—he is ludicrous and obtusely inhuman by remaining in his office, quietly reflective and engrossed, entirely absorbed by his literary work. He is innocent, because he still doesn't know the war has started, and is legitimately devoting himself to writing, to polishing a sentence, deleting one adjective too many. But the simple fact that his wife and daughter, two women of remarkable culture and intelligence, can for even a moment think that they should not disturb him and that he might be annoyed by it makes this story a tragic farce, transforming the sacrosanct respect for his brilliant work into an unintentional parody, like wondering whether a king should wear the crown on his head when going to bed or to the toilet.

November 25, 2011

A ROSE OF THE BLESSED

In the Cathedral of Saint Nicholas, in Saint Petersburg—the province is still called Leningrad—just to the right as you enter is a painting, a large panel with several panes, all, of course, depicting religious subjects and marked by the enchanting fixity of icons, not the rigid arrest of time but an eternity of moments full of grace and meaning, which transcend time and its passing

A central pane depicts a procession of saints, a long line that recedes and grows smaller, anonymous and obscure travelers on their way. The first ones, gazing directly at the viewer, look very much alike, just as for us—at least, according to a popular saying that is increasingly belied—all Chinese look somewhat alike; they are obviously dressed the same, wearing a monk's cowl, and each of them has a halo because they are saints, men on whom a higher grace shines, the essential light. But their marked features, if you observe them closely, are different; each face has its own unique expression, a gentler or more determined gaze, a firmer or more smiling mouth. They are individuals, very similar yet each one distinct.

Behind them, the host of pilgrims becomes, in perspective, more and more uniform, the individual figures smaller and smaller, more and more indistinguishable. On their heads the golden halo is an increasingly pure and luminous gold that shines and flickers eternally; toward the end they are all so many halos fused into a single brilliance, though each, albeit narrowly, with its form and individuality. One is reminded of the Celestial Rose of the blessed in Dante's *Paradiso*, perhaps also of the vacuity espoused by Buddhism: a condition in which the individual, in his essence, still exists and indeed exists in his essential purity, but liberated from the ego, both from his inessential and idolatrously pursued resolves and from his self-centered arrogance.

Being individuals in that procession no longer involves the sorrow of being separate from the universe and from the flow of life, or the frantic, self-destructive desire to be dissolved in the undifferentiated ocean of the Whole. It means being a brother among brothers, without whom a man would not be what he is; a voice in a choir, unmistakable and necessary but that only exists if it harmonizes with that choir, which, conversely, is absolutely in need of it. "Ecce quam bonum et quam jucundum habitare fratres in Unum," Scripture says, "Behold how good and how pleasant it is for brethren to dwell together in unity." But perhaps, to be one of those wayfarers, all it takes is to fall in love, a nice infatuation that helps us find ourselves outside of ourselves, in someone else's life. Certain tresses, not only blond ones, are in no way less luminous than those halos.

April 14, 2012

THE DEVIL'S DUNG

Under a tent in the courtyard of an elegant palazzo in Friuli, hastily and efficiently erected against the looming chance of rain in this capricious month of June, discussions center on the economic crisis, on the decline of capitalism leading to it, on the prospects and high or low probabilities of recovering from it, and on various great and not so great leading figures of the Italian economy, staunch defenders of legality and equity or blatant liars and profiteers. The speakers on the platform, four of them, adhere strictly to the facts; they try—especially one, the meeting's organizer—to clarify things, to explain the difference between a sound economy based primarily on production and an economy focused foolishly on financial speculations based on nothing, just so many inflated zeros that at first seem like something and in the end prove to be what they are, zeros. Someone rightly points out that the feverish quest for money, disconnected from a real context of work and human relations, becomes a distortion of life.

To the audience, a public composed mainly of affluent individuals rather than victims of the crisis robbed of a secure future, it is of little interest to understand whether the crisis, as the speakers are trying to analyze, is a pathological degeneration of capitalism due to the errors, sins, and misdeeds of single albeit numerous parties or to economic forces, and therefore a culpable and preventable malady, or the physiological, inexorable senescence of the system, like the decline of an empire. The audience instead seems eager to hear the speakers decry money, in the broadest, most general sense possible, and to look back nostalgically on the "good old days" when we were poor and therefore—according to this false view portrayed by Edmondo De Amicis's novel *Cuore* (Heart)—happier. At some point—even in chats after the session, drinking excellent champagne, and eating superb prosciutto—it seems that for many, money is the medieval Devil's dung.

I try in vain to make it clear to an elderly gentleman, apparently from a high social bracket, that the problem today, in Italy and other countries (or rather for the vast majority of their citizens, aside from a privileged few or the corrupt), is not an excess of money but its scarcity. In the good old days—which ones were they? those of arduous factory work during the Industrial Revolution, of agricultural laborers with no protection, of the brutal exploitation of minors?—almost everyone was much, much worse off, just as, in the vast world, millions and millions of people are worse off than we are today, living like so many of our ancestors did in bygone centuries. For the elderly gentleman and for many others beside him, glass in hand, the good old days.

The shameless, rightly deplored fever of extreme consumption needs to reapply its makeup, powdering its face with the simplicity of ancient times, rustic authenticity, austerity of customs. Triumphant, blatant capitalism wears the veil (every now and then, for a few minutes) of modesty and would ennoble itself with the cosmetics of a medievalizing, romantic anti-capitalism, incited by Adam Smith as well as by Marx. It is a hypocrisy absolutely in good faith and therefore even worse, because it corrupts not only the heart but also the intelligence.

This nostalgia for "good" poverty does not lessen the objection to taxes, which inasmuch as they lighten the pockets should therefore, according to this view, purify existence. To those at the cocktail reception who mourn for the old days of indigence, I say that I am ready to shoulder a little of the curse of their wealth and to provide my IBAN for any wire transfers of that burden. But this generous offer of mine unfortunately is met with — in this case the expression is appropriate — deaf ears.

June 16, 2012

THE BEAUTIFUL SUMMER

A summer day on an island in the Quarnero (Kvarner); one of those utterly perfect days, whose maritime beauty bestows a sense of exaltation but also a sharp pang because, as has been said of love, it makes us aware of everything that we don't have. It is a Saturday, a day of turnover, as some tourists leave and other tourists arrive to replace them, like the rotating *cinquantine* — groups of fifty girls — in the days of brothels. The ordeal of those departing is the dread of long lines of cars that mean hours of not moving, waiting for the ferry, in the sun and jarring heat. A sudden stoppage of the cars up ahead, inching along the high road overlooking the sea, enthralling though tortuous and unsuitable for passing, is troublesome, threatening possible interminable holdups. People get out of their cars, drinking from their bottles, walk toward the first curve to see what happened. But after the first curve come countless others that prevent knowing the state of things; from people farther on bits and pieces of news and hypotheses make their way up and down, deformed in passing from one voice to another, as in the old game of Telephone.

A woman gets out of a car. No longer young, decidedly beautiful in her elegant, generous curves that reveal a hearty zest for living, even if the heat is not very gallant toward that lovely flesh: sweat plows fleeting furrows like wrinkles and softens the buxom arms and cheeks. A man, who appears to be informed, is getting back into his car. The woman goes over to him. "A long backup, are we stuck?" she asks him. "No," the man replies, "it's an accident. There's someone hurt, lying on the ground; as soon as the ambulance comes, we'll be on our way again." "Thank goodness," the woman says, relieved, as she walks back to her car. The others are silent, grateful that she has borne the burden of saying what they think, what we're all thinking.

July 9, 2012

WRITING, ENTRY PROHIBITED

At the Coroneo prison in Trieste, talking with inmates. About reading and literature, according to the agenda, but soon enough about other, more burning issues as well. I introduce the meeting trying to describe how a book comes about, to suggest the reasons that lead to writing, the relationship between author and reader. At one point a detainee who is serving a harsh sentence for murder says that, like his fellow prisoners, he too writes, adding, however, that as far as writing is concerned, there is an unbridgeable difference between them and me and my colleagues committed to literary homelands. *You authors*, he says, *write to publish, to communicate, to convey to others what you feel inside; for me and others like me in this prison, the reasons that lead us to write are just the opposite. We write — at least in my case*, he says, *but I know the same applies to others — to have at least one thing that is ours, ours alone, not subject to the scrutiny that exposes every shred of our lives and our experience to an X-ray. In here I have nothing that is mine, mine alone; my existence is made to be stripped, searched, recorded. What I write, on the other hand, is only mine; I don't show it to anyone, I would never want anyone to read it, it is my world where the jailers, the law, the judges, the inmates, and all the others cannot enter. And on that paper I feel free, without guards, with no one to rob me of myself.*

Evidently for that man, laying bare his heart, as the title of a work by Baudelaire says, would mean undergoing further violation. I don't think he is right. Writing, communicating, giving a part of yourself to others can be a gesture of generosity, a gift, that opens a dialogue. And it is primarily in dialogue, in coming out of oneself and encountering the other, that the meaning of existence is found. Moreover, in other prisons—for example, in Bollate, in Bergamo, or in Viterbo—other detainees, they too devoted to writing, have told me the opposite, expressing a desire to speak in that way with someone. But in that man's obstinate determination to isolate himself in his cell at Coroneo, there is also a truth, a need for privacy and a will to resist which everyone ought to have, even those who are not behind bars.

I look at him, I listen to him, and I think about the lewd spiritual striptease that has become more and more widespread. About lovers or ex-lovers eager to expose their acrimonies on television, debasing the bed to the level of backstairs squabbling and scandal; about mothers whose heart in hand overwhelms the screen; about the legions on Facebook who reveal intimacies—no more interesting than their underwear—to people they don't know, who remain even more unrelated after the exchange, or who obscenely spread intimacies stolen from others. Even the heart, writes Flaubert, has its latrines, but you don't see them because you have to peep at these latrines through a keyhole, inviting thousands of others to do so, or because you have to open the door of your own latrine while evacuating, inviting others to watch.

Then again I also think about those of us who write and not only publish but go around, perhaps not baring our hearts but certainly putting them in the spotlight, reading our work aloud, hoping for crowds of listeners, telling how and why we filled these folios with words, what noble, deeply felt, or transgressive passions lie behind those printed pages. Naturally we hope that people will admire the darkness we put on display, not realizing that by so doing, as Borges writes in a memorable passage, we drain ourselves, we let everything be taken from us, and that dark space inside us is in danger of remaining empty.

We will not try to be like the inmate who so rigidly guards his darkness; it would not be right and, above all, we would not be capable of it. We are unable to refuse to open our hearts to the attendees who stand in line waiting for opening time. People whose generosity is often more profound, intelligent, and genuine than ours. But if only we wouldn't bare this heart completely; if only we would, out of decency, put some kind of shirt on it, not necessarily striped.

November 1, 2012

DOWN WITH THE POOR

A session of the Trieste city council, years ago. The topic under discussion is subsidized gasoline, a privilege that, to compensate for the competition of cheaper-priced fuel across the nearby border, has for years enabled Triestines to buy gas at more advantageous prices than in other regions, obviously at the expense of Italian taxpayers. Franco Panizon, a brilliant pediatrician who is great with children, unacquainted with what the church disapproves of as a lack of courage in expressing one's own opinions, and aware that in every ward or hospital room there is the world, sits on the side of the left. Like the children he treats, he is a man who has maintained the extraordinary creativity of childhood, the ability to play, that is, to do the most spontaneous, uninhibited thing in the world. Once he showed me a child, who would die a few days later, who was playing with a big, unwieldy device that administered his IV drip, running and sliding with it as if it were a bumper car at an amusement park.

Proving that the left is sometimes more liberal and liberalistic than the right (at that time the majority on the city council), Franco Panizon declares that he is opposed to that privilege, seeing no good reason why a Calabrian or Ligurian citizen should pay taxes so that he can drive around the Karst a little more cheaply. The mayor observes acidly that the Councilman of the Left Panizon is not very sensitive to the needs of the poor. At which Panizon stands up and shouts, "Down with the poor!" Indeed, a decent person would not want there to be any poor, would not want anyone to be poor. So it went in Trieste, on a late afternoon some years ago.

November 16, 2012

THE RIGHT WORD IN THE WRONG MOUTH

I think it was Karl Kraus who coined the expression "The worst thing is the right word in the wrong mouth." For example—though these examples are too easy—the word *homeland* in the mouth of a nationalist or *God* in the mouth of a hypocrite, or *mother* in the mouth of a speaker at a Family Day rally, or *diversity* tossed out at a demonstration. Kraus's quip came to mind a few days ago on the train, as I was seeing and unavoidably listening to the conversation of a couple sitting in front of me in the compartment. They must have been a pair whose marriage, whether lawful or de facto, was not their first, with other families behind them and at least some children not in common.

The man looked concerned, worried about someone evidently closer to him than to his well-groomed partner. Perhaps a daughter, named shortly before, in any case a young female person, as could be deduced by the nature of the anxieties from which, I gathered, she was clearly suffering; these distressed the man and above all left him disoriented, making him unsure how to respond to the many manifestations of those anxieties—listen to them, assume their burden, or confront them firmly or even severely so as not to exacerbate them by giving them too much leeway. He was disconcerted; he seemed unable to distinguish a cry for help due to profound suffering from the obsessive, egocentric demand that sometimes accompanies it. There is the brutal indifference or irritation of the healthy toward the sick, and there is the conspiracy of the sick against the healthy.

The man, agitated, groped about trying to understand which behavior was the right one, more useful to the person he cared so much about and whose difficulties unsettled him. He too was asking for help and guidance, and his companion—at least, as far as seat assignments on the train were concerned—counseled him with brisk resolve. From what I could hear, in my indiscreet but unavoidable eavesdropping, her opinions were correct and intelligent. She gave him advice and orders about acting strict, brusque, and even fed up, which in her opinion would serve to defuse the situation and make it clear to the girl that her anxieties were groundless, thereby helping her take them less seriously and not suffer so much. The words were essentially right, appropriate to the situation, useful instructions. But the mouth that uttered them—a pretty mouth, but tense and hardened—gave them a tone that canceled out or upended their meaning and effect, the way a room with bad acoustics spoils the music that is played there. There was, on that mouth, no anguished albeit steadfast sympathy for her companion's dismay or for the suffering, real though perhaps overly hyper, of the person so dear to him. The set of those lips did not suggest a severity reluctantly assumed because it was deemed necessary and useful; on those lips, instead, was a hint of unwitting spite, a dissatisfaction often linked to malice, the infantile, hurtful meanness of a child toward the cry of a companion on whom he or she has inflicted a small cruelty, innocent and malicious.

Perhaps the man, at that moment weak and irresolute, was in

other circumstances strong and decisive, a dominant presence, and Delilah wasn't too unhappy about cutting off Samson's hair, seeing him fettered by his own weakness. Her mouth wasn't even pretty anymore, the way a cruel, rapacious or perverse mouth can be, though not a mouth on which malevolence hovers. So the woman's intelligent, correct words, which could have helped the man better deal with the anxiety that filled him, became useless and harmful, because to be truly right and supportive they would have had to share his anguish, not indulging it but shouldering it and making it their own. But to do that they would have had to come out, exactly as they were, from a different mouth. Better the opposite, better the wrong words in the right mouth, I thought, watching them stand up, together yet apart, to get off the train a few stops before mine.

January 23, 2013

SEA LION

Trieste, Barcola riviera. On the rocky strip that runs along viale Miramare, the avenue leading into the city, and at the small public swimming facilities, the so-called "Topolini," one or two people are diving or lying out in the wan sunshine of a windy day, but the shore is practically deserted. An elderly portly man in a bathing suit is dozing with a newspaper in his hand; some distance away a young girl comes out of the water. A group of guys appear, interchangeable in their vaguely threatening bawdiness, and start harassing the girl. Up to a certain point the situation remains within the limits of an annoying, moronic vulgarity, then the action starts to heat up, hands reach out, the girl is a little scared, and the casual observer begins to worry that he will have to step in, wondering how he'll be able to do it.

Fortunately for him, as well as for the girl, the portly gentleman gets up, revealing a substantial paunch, and tells the herd to stop it. The young men approach him, rowdy and aggressive, making as if to shove him and vulgarly tell him not to look for trouble. The gentleman promptly stands with his back to the wall, lifts the heavy marble pedestal of a beach umbrella with only one hand, sets it down on the ground with apparent ease and motions the guys to come forward. "Come on," he says, "the first one gets smashed against the wall, after that, have no fear, I'll tear you to pieces, all of you. Well, who's first?" The gang mutters menacing obscenities and gradually backs away, not too fast, to save face, and with a blustering air, as if they were letting it go out of kindness. The girl has meanwhile disappeared. The most relieved and happy of all is the casual observer, overjoyed that he was not put to the test.

The elderly man lies down and goes back to reading; at one point he gets up, walks toward the sea. But at that moment his wife shows up, who had apparently gone to do some shopping and is unaware of the match that was avoided. "Alberto!" she shouts peremptorily. "Don't tell me you're going to take a swim with the water so cold, and no sun, totally oblivious as usual!" The man raises his head, opens his mouth to reply, then changes his mind and retraces his steps, sadly turning his back to the sea. "I told you not to take off your undershirt! And never mind that cigarette, anyway we're going home now, it's late; dear God, have a little good sense, you're worse than a child."

The man gets dressed, looks at the sea, then the woman. His eyes, which meet mine for a moment as I walk by him to get to the water, are veiled and remind me of those of a lion I once saw in a circus, staring at the people in front of its cage with a resigned awareness of not being able to devour them and probably also with the sad conviction that it was only right not to. The gentleman and his wife start back to the car. Farther away, the gang from before is horsing around in the sea, smacking and slapping one another on the back, scuffling to shove each other's heads underwater. The man watches them, perhaps with envy.

July 1, 2013

JENS'S GRAVESTONE

Blue, along with gold and white, dominates even the ceiling and the walls of the small church of Dypvåg, in southern Norway, which dates back to the twelfth century. Blue, the color of distance and longing, is fitting for Norway. The parish church of Dypvåg— "one of the oldest and most beautiful in all of Norway," reads the brochure, a safe haven for the body and soul of fishermen and sailors—has, despite restorations and renovations, the sturdy, spare grace of the wooden churches scattered throughout the country, a house of God but primarily of families and individuals whose piety encompasses not only prayer but also and especially the work of hands skilled in shaping wood, building houses and boats with a close understanding of the direction of the wind and movements of the currents. There are paintings by excellent artists, a pulpit and a baldachin displaying a plainspoken solemnity.

In front of the old church there is, as there should be, a cemetery, which pertains to it not for reasons of religious concession but because it contains the world and lives of the local people. It is not surprising that in many Germanic languages the cemetery is called the churchyard. Our cemeteries are cities, necropolises and metropolises of marble, majestic triumphs of death and its order; they call to mind building speculation rather than eternal life. In Scandinavian countries, as in others, gravestones, nearly always small and inconspicuous in size, are scattered randomly among the trees; some practically concealed in the grass, an understory of names and dates. No pretentious family chapel with cupolas and columns, which here would be as ridiculous as a king in bed with the crown on his head. A place for walks, for family closeness, in which even the word *death* sounds too pompous. Gravestones and stone crosses bear the names of fishermen and farmers, merchants and seamen, and the builders of sailing vessels that created the prosperity of nearby Risør, later challenged by steamships but soon recovered. The trim, stately yet sober homes of the shipowners of the past and of today are a distillate of this extraordinary rural and seafaring country that has produced one of the most disconcerting literatures of modern disintegration; a country that was very poor a century ago and today is the richest in the world, with not a cent of public debt.

On the gravestones, names and dates of birth and death summarize, with essentiality and discretion, the existence of their occupants. Near a huge plant is a small gravestone, or rather a vaguely roundish stone about eight inches in diameter. There is a name, Jens Keilon, and a single date: July 26, 1993, evidently the day of birth and also of death. That individual lived for only twenty-four hours. What could have happened in those twenty-four hours? His life is more interesting, in part because it is more hidden and unknown, than that of the other parishioners around him. I wonder if the time he lived was merely the misfortune or series of misfortunes that interrupted his journey, or if there was also joy, the inarticulate but no less passionate recognition of a mother already well known to him and reencountered in a different way and with a different face. His life is a totality, no less so than those of the others beside him; a small, very tiny existence in the world's flow, minimal but absolute and unique. Compared to the vast labyrinth of things that make up the world, history, the universe, and even the lives of those who die at forty or eighty years of age, this one is absurdly irrelevant, a drop in an ocean, yet inimitable and matchless.

I think about Jens, about how the arc of his life intersected with that of the world. That day, July 26, 1993, the *Corriere della sera* reports the funeral of Raul Gardini, who committed suicide for fear of being arrested for alleged embezzlement, and news of a South Korean Boeing that crashed in Seoul resulting in sixty-three deaths, while an article by Alfio Sciacca recounts and comments on word of a judge who had asked the mob to shoot a teacher who had failed his nephew. Shiite militias attack Lebanon, two boys die in an accident in Milan, fierce protests are raised in the United States against sentencing to death a dog guilty of having bitten a child. Every life, even the most unknown and rejected, is linked in the world to all the others. Life is a chorale, especially in the final moment that sums it up

The newspaper, on that July 26, 1993, does not mention Jens, or President Clinton either. About Jens one could say that he cried, even loudly, when emerging from the womb to the outside world; that he sucked, though perhaps not actual breast milk yet, and probably that he wailed, rightly so, far more than he could realize. Perhaps, at some moment, held in the arms or with his mouth on the nipple, that he was also happy. But even if they had written his biography, it would have been an incomplete biography, relative to the final phase, because Jens did not live one day only, but nine months plus one day, and during those nine months he swam, he heard voices that perhaps for him spelled happiness, he kicked vigorously. He lived, even though he did not have a chance to be aware of his life, to be rationally conscious of it. But in this, perhaps, he was not very different from many of his contemporaries and travel companions along the incomprehensible ways of the world, who on that day could read their names and maybe see their ultrasound, I mean photograph, in the paper.

July 30, 2013

MUTE SCENES OF A MARRIAGE

At the table of a tavern in the Triestine Karst, friends who came to enjoy some fresh air ironically observe a couple at another table, probably husband and wife. Sitting opposite one another, glasses in front of them, the two do not exchange a word, each fiddling with an iPhone or other such device; from time to time they speak, not with their companion but with invisible interlocutors, though generally they are silent, absorbed in themselves and in their gadgets. A few years ago they would probably have erected a newspaper between them, a paper Iron Curtain now replaced by newer, more sophisticated insulating walls.

At the other table a contemptuous smile is de rigueur and underscores the pleasure of finding fault with the times and the decline of authentic human relationships. Single people, in particular, are gratified to experience firsthand the boredom of marriage, the distance that creeps between a long-standing couple. In general there is the satisfaction of criticizing the banality and stereotypical behavior of others—it is always others who are banal—of feeling that one is free from conventionality and deadly routine, an authentic soul quick to spot others everywhere who are not so and to pity them, criticize them, correct them, free them from the mechanical repetition of their lives, teach them how to live. In every severe critic of humdrum banality is a schoolteacher, maybe one of those from earlier times, with a ruler in hand.

Which table's occupants are the most successful? Every so often the two presumed spouses, albeit fleetingly, glance at each other; an instant of serene, mysterious tenderness. Once she touches his arm lightly. Why, in order to be more genuine, would she have to shut down her digital device, which in no way detracts from that caress? And why should being together in silence always be a sign of desolation and distance? Of course, estrangement can be a sting of unhappiness and rob people—especially when they are people who love each other or who once loved each other or who realize sadly that they love each other but are mutually incompatible—of that dialogue in which we only truly exist.

But the ruthless, inhuman workings of reality too often deprive us of another blessing: solitude, our need to be alone, to live at least occasionally in the Far West of our heart, where we are sometimes truly ourselves only if we are alone, like the cowboy in the old westerns. To love also means to understand and protect the solitude which the other person requires; understand that he or she may not want to dine at home, not just because he has a dull yet respected working lunch that does no harm to any marriage but because that day he needs to be alone with his own thoughts and lose himself in their vagabond drifting. Instead, a line from Rilke says, "Lovers tread constantly on each other's boundaries."[14]

The two presumed spouses at that table therefore have no duty to become loquacious, nor do others have a right to know if they are happy or unhappy, if and how they love each other, what, if any, wrongs they have inflicted on each other. Human truth is also the respect of this opacity, an inalienable right of everyone, though one that is constantly violated. Why this craving to probe into the lives of others, trying to put them through an X-ray machine, demanding to know the truth about them and often actually tainting them by buzzing around them, always convinced of doing so for their sake, though they may well prefer that we mind our own business? As Don Quixote says, let each man answer for his own sins.[15]

August 23, 2013

EVERYTHING'S ALL RIGHT

In Schio, a Saturday night. The Italian Manchester, it was called until a few years ago, when the textile industry made the small town a thriving center of the passionate, earthy, unsophisticated Veneto, an example of how sensuality and dedication can get along together, vigorous work and a cynical sweet life. Now the crisis has partly drained the prosperous town of money and cheer, fabrics are made in China. I dine alone in a pizzeria. There is only one other customer. He eats staring straight ahead of him. If it were not for him, the room would simply be a physical space, temporarily empty, that does neither good nor harm to anyone. Instead his presence, his inaccessible remoteness, and his blank stare aimed at the wall fill it with an infinite, disconsolate loneliness. Sometimes one is never so alone as when there are two. A small sacred tableau of the exile from Eden.

I go out to smoke my cigar. The night is damp, a few harmless drops trickle from the air. I sit on the sidewalk, smoking. A small group of young people pass by, a few of them from some African country. As they walk by, one of the latter, with an accent already nearly Venetian, leans toward me and asks, "Everything all right?" Evidently my age, for one thing, along with my not particularly elegant but unmistakably respectable bourgeois suit and raincoat, make that posture dubious. I reassure them, even though the expression "everything's all right," taken literally, could be a tough one, debatable. We chat a bit, one tells me that he comes from Senegal, a girl born and raised in nearby Thiene is a barista. It occurs to me that I have never asked, "Everything all right?" of someone squatting on the ground. The kids move off, laughing. It was a really nice evening, I think with gratitude as I get up and head for the hotel, and their evening, as it should be, will probably be even nicer. Everything's all right.

June 12, 2014

AT THE WINDOW

The Cemeteries Office of the city of Trieste. The line of people who, though not yet the end users, are for various reasons inquiring about a final resting place—presumably for persons more or less dearly beloved who have passed on to a better life and are in need of suitable accommodation or, as required by law after a certain number of years, of being moved (urn, niche, mass grave)—is small. A city with few births and therefore few deaths.

The physical proximity of the gentleman in front of me who has already arrived at the window makes it inevitable that I indiscreetly overhear what the two are saying, the citizen and the clerk at his service. Something—some detail, a procedural error, a missing document—connected with the evidently recent departure of the man's father, not yet returned to the earth, at least in a literal sense. I understand that the grave that awaits him—and there is some discussion about the reasons for the protracted wait—is a family plot. The two argue back and forth; the orphan, though by age more than suited to that state, objects to something, the other responds by appealing to records, stamps, signatures. At one point the clerk, slightly exasperated but always with the decorous, indifferent regard owed to someone else's death, asks again who the owner or owners of the grave may be. "It belongs to my father," the man replies. The clerk looks up, leans slightly forward through the window, closer to the man's face. "I'm sorry to tell you," he says coldly, "your father is no longer the owner of anything." One definition of death as good as another. At school, the catechism instructor spoke instead of "separation of the soul from the body."

July 10, 2014

FRECCIABIANCA

On the high-speed Milan-Trieste Frecciabianca, in the afternoon. Somewhere behind me a dog barks occasionally. It's not a great nuisance, the travelers in fact do not protest; they turn to glance around, some more annoyed, others with good-natured irony.

The conductor comes by and asks the dog owner to silence the animal and also to change cars, since she has a second-class ticket; the woman has a wizened face, an unchanging expression, absent and indifferent. She is clearly disturbed, probably impaired by alcohol as well. She seems not to understand what is being said to her and is reluctant; she refuses to leave. The conductor raises his voice and pushes her. Slurring her words she asks him to show her his ID, he shouts, she swears at him in strong, vulgar terms, he's seized by a real fit of rage, swears back at her with even stronger and more vulgar words; she stares into space and repeats her profanity, he, convulsed and furious, red-faced, yells that he's going to break every bone in her body even if it means going to jail. The passengers watch, we look at one another, dumbfounded, wondering vaguely if we should intervene and who will be the one to do it, held back by the universal cowardice that leads us to ignore even much more serious situations, embarrassed. The dog, more dignified than the two contenders, minds his own business.

Only one lady, closer to the degrading scene, tries to step in, gently urging the woman toward the door of the car, amid her muttered obscenities and the conductor's shouts and threats. The woman finally leaves, and we later come to learn that she was made to get off in Desenzano. The conductor passes back through the car and mumbles a few words of apology. Maybe he's exasperated by the countless other distressing, taxing incidents that happen to him each day, which can be infuriating. Ensuring compliance with the law is more demanding than violating it. As for the woman, who knows what miseries, rejections, perhaps assaults have marked her lifeless, withered face, making her look like an impassive Indian, much older than her age? What a lot of sorrows life, that malevolent engraver, etches on our faces.

December 11, 2014

GRAFFITI

Berlin. The taxi that takes me from the airport to the hotel gets stopped for a few minutes, caught in an abrupt traffic jam in Invalidenstrasse, at number 86. On the wall of the building someone has spray-painted in large letters: "Ne lisez jamais!" A peremptory, passionate urging—for some reason in French—not to read, not to ever read.

I doubt that its anonymous author is a belated follower of those gleeful students who in 1968 publicly tore up books as an expression of (false and repressive) bourgeois culture. Perhaps this too is intended to be, in its way, a cry for freedom, though more distressing. Freedom from reading—and consequently, prior to that, writing—accused of fixing and suspending life, distorting the truth of the instant, the inimitable word of the moment. It's not surprising that the great masters of humanity—Christ, Socrates, Buddha—did not write, did not choose to write; perhaps because the truth they proclaimed was uniquely and irreproducibly linked to the person speaking it, to the concrete authenticity of the moment and of the state of mind in which it was spoken. Can you imagine Jesus or Buddha writing a book, revising the proofs, and delivering them to the editor?

It was others who wrote and enabled their words to be read, their faithful followers who not only listened but also repeated and handed down their words, detaching them from the immediacy of how they resounded under the trees of India or in the streets of Galilee. Of course, reading the story of a life is not the same as experiencing it or witnessing it, hearing words that touch the heart as they come out of a mouth. But those words nourish us thanks to those who suspended them and transcribed them. When you come right down to it, that Francophone iconoclast also wrote his words and passersby read them.

April 3, 2015

ADVERTISING, A LONG, TEDIOUS SERMON

In the era of secularization, advertising sometimes replaces the gloom-and-doom preachers of the so-called dark ages, scourges of the flesh smugly pleased to remind us that under glorious breasts is a skeleton destined to crumble into dust. Advertising also takes steps, as is only fair, to spoil other pleasures with its warnings. The viewer watching a thriller, a sappy soap opera, or a news feature on television is interrupted, maybe just when he is about to discover the killer, by other stories that burst on the screen. Brief commercials starring beautiful women who sweat, perspire, smell, leak fluids from their most delicate parts, have greasy, oily hair and bad breath in mouths that are inviting to the eye but apparently repellent to the olfactory organ.

Dramas that fortunately have a quick, happy ending, because ephemeral but repetitive redeemers will immediately appear on the screen: lotions, potions, creams, oils, ointments, patches, sprays; those bodies will once more flourish, become seductive and inviting again, and soon afterward the viewer will go back to watching his detective film.

Dramas with happy endings, but not for long. Whereas religion, ignored, proclaims that splendid flesh "glorious" and promises it a final resurrection, the viewer in front of the television is soon interrupted again, and those bodies — not only women but also, though to a lesser extent, men, as equal opportunity dictates — are again sweaty, damp, shamefully wet and malodorous. It must be recognized that television advertising, though it is certainly a bane that ruins the decent pastime of those who would like to watch a program, is also a great Lenten sermon, heir to the universality of medieval Mystery plays in which all beauty, wealth, and power end in ashes. If there were no manufacturers of deodorants, depilatories, tampons, and shampoos, who would still remember that we are destined to turn to dust?

August 22, 2015

THE ROCKY BEACH OF THE FAMOUS

Here I know who I am, said Julius Kugy, the great mountaineer as well as spirited writer and organist from Gorizia, when he was in his Julian Alps. Certain places are sometimes virtually one with our persona; they are a modality of our relationship with the world. Places signify landscapes, natural or manmade or better yet both, the lake and the cottage on its shore inseparable in a poem by Brecht.[16] Places especially signify people, more or less familiar or nearly strangers but in any case witnesses, albeit partial, of our existence.

One such place for me is the rocky strip in Barcola, bordering the road that runs along the sea at the entrance to Trieste, from where you can dive freely in waters that quickly become deep. A place that for me is identified with summer, the true season of life—when I read the novels of James Fenimore Cooper I really liked the fact that his Mohicans counted their years by calling them "summers" instead of "springs." Even a modest beach at the edge of an open sea can become a theater of the world, such as years ago, when a man died of a heart attack in the water and, dragged to the shore to wait for the ambulance, lay there dead for a long time, under a sheet, among the other bathers lying beside him suntanning or sitting playing cards.

That place too is made up mostly of people, more or less the same ones, who each day claim the same spot that has practically become an acquired right, and who little by little are woven, albeit superficially, into the tapestry of a common life, not quite but almost like a class at school. It is therefore not so strange when someone, lying in the sun or coming out of the water, is occasionally recognized and maybe, even if he is not Hemingway, asked to sign a book. But the other day things unfolded in a different, more gratifying way. "*Xe Suo 'sto can*, is this your dog?" a lady asked in dialect, pointing to Jackson, my little Brussels Griffon, essential companion of my life, who also loves the sea, although, over the years, more and more calmly. To my affirmative answer, the lady replied, "Then you must be Claudio Magris." Now I too, thanks to Jackson, know who I am.

October 2, 2015

THE SIN OF ACRIMONY

Easter mass in Aurisina, Nabrežina in Slovenian, a lively little village in the Karst in the province of Trieste. The parish priest in his homily speaks of resurrection, that of Christ and the interior resurrection offered to each of us, the spiritual rebirth that should renew an individual and give him joy, as Jesus prescribes: "May your joy be complete." But as I look around, as I look at you—the priest continues, leaning forward from the pulpit a bit—I do not see faces of resurrection, but rather troubled, petulant, grumpy faces.

The priest is right to reproach our sulky faces, more frustrated and mistrustful than open and joyful. He knows that many reasons, personal and collective, may cast a shadow on a face and mark it with spiritual scars—sorrows, anxieties, illness, loneliness, difficulties of all kinds. He is certainly not rebuking the suffering of his flock, because he knows that faith is called upon to alleviate and combat the wounds of body and heart and may sometimes result from those wounds. But the impervious acrimony on our faces is more than an expression of pain or sorrow. It is the bitter resentment of those who seethe over what they don't have rather than rejoice over what they do have; of the deputy director not yet promoted to director who, despite his more conspicuous salary, is more sullenly unsatisfied than the employees who report to him; of the writer who is resentful because he received one award but not another more prestigious one; of the partner who feels misunderstood and doesn't stop to ask, as almost none of us do, whether it might be him or her who doesn't understand the other. Resentment, the great philosophers have said, is sometimes key to the story, individual and general.

Unwittingly, the priest is rightly reassessing physiognomy, often justly reviled for some of its racist implications. There is a kind of sourness—*da mal de panza*, as they say in Trieste, as when you have a belly ache—that is not always the painful experience of sorrow, but a proud refusal to feel understood and satisfied, unlike the character recalled by Isaac Bashevis Singer in his memoirs of childhood, a poor devil whose face "always wore a joyous, holiday look of contentment."[17] Maximus the Confessor, a Christian theologian and martyr of the seventh century, said that glumness and melancholy sometimes conceal conscious or unconscious rancor. The great religious faiths are quite familiar with the abyss of despair, with desperation's bloody sweat, but they don't wallow in them; instead they love joyfulness: Buddhist serenity, Franciscan elation, the Seer of Lublin, an Eastern Jewish holy man, who loved an unrepentant sinner because the latter, despite repeated falls, had preserved his joy intact.

Ite Missa est, go in peace, the mass is ended. Only when you can laugh again, said an inscription I'd read more than thirty years ago on the door of the Linz cathedral, have you really forgiven.

April 14, 2016

UNTRANSLATABLE

Snapshot of a walk on the Karst a few weeks ago. A lapidary apologue for translators, an epiphany of their great, impossible work. In a Karstic doline two children, under the watchful eye of their grandfather, are playing, constantly devising unpredictable adventures. The boy—his name is Isaac—is two years and some months old, the grandfather proudly tells me; the brown skin and curly hair of a child of parents of different color, bright, gentle, mischievous eyes, brimming with intelligence and joie de vivre. He clambers up a tree, falls, gets up laughing, makes himself a club or a rifle out of a branch, tries to whistle into a reed, chases a bird that moves slightly ahead of his charge. The girl's name is Vera, radiant white and shy as a daisy, with sweet blue eyes; she's one year old, looks around spellbound, astonished, and sometimes intimidated by the world that her cousin with the captivating dark skin conquers, rushing into the fray and shouting, "Charge!"

Every so often she stumbles in the thick, damp grass, and he, a big-hearted swaggerer, immediately runs to help her up; if his grandfather gives him a cookie, he gives her a piece of it and resumes the rounds of his colonies. It's clear that the world is his and that he opens it up magnanimously to others without losing the sense of owning life. Perhaps happiness is none other than that sovereignty. When his grandfather, looking up at the sky that is clearing after the rain that recently stopped, says to himself, in a voice barely intelligible to those around him, "Viene primavera," spring is coming, the boy, who was running, stops, turns to him, and says, gently but firmly, "No, prima Isacco," Isaac comes first.

Unwitting and untranslatable brilliance. Translation, an old Triestine manual said, is impossible but essential.

May 8, 2016

Death was instantaneous.

—Aldo Palazzeschi

TRANSLATOR'S NOTES

1. An *osmiza* is a private home offering fresh meats, cheeses, and wines that the occupants themselves produce.

2. The line is from "Le Cygne, II,": "Widow of Hector, alas! and wife of Helenus!" Charles Baudelaire, "The Swan, II," in *The Flowers of Evil*, trans. William Aggeler (Fresno, Calif.: Academy Library Guild, 1954).

3. *Morra* is a hand game, similar to Rock—Paper—Scissors.

4. The story is "Lazarus," by Leonid N. Andreyev.

5. Italy, originally allied with Germany in World War II, surrendered to the Allies on September 8, 1943. Germany then invaded Italy.

6. The IRCCS (Istituto di ricovero e cura a carattere scientifico) is an institute dedicated to in-patient treatment and scientific studies.

7. "O blessed solitude! O sole beatitude!" is attributed to Saint Bernard of Clairvaux.

8. "Ah Pippo mio, quant'era mejo / se pagavi la tassa su li scapoli!" From the sonnet *"Er marito infelice"* by Trilussa (Carlo Alberto Salustri), a twentieth-century Roman dialect poet.

9. The last stanza of the French singer-songwriter and poet Georges Brassens's "Les Passantes" reads, "On pleure les lèvres absentes / De toutes ces belles passantes / Que l'on n'a pas su retenir" (One weeps for lips, sadly absent, / Of all those beaut'ful passersby / Whom you knew not how to keep hold of).

10. Vladimir Ilyich Lenin's *What Is to Be Done? Burning Ques-*

tions of Our Movement, a political pamphlet, written in 1901 and published in 1902.

11. Half a liter = 1 cup; 300 grams = 10 oz.; 75 grams = 3 oz.; 100 grams = 3.5 oz.

12. For centuries, the *Index librorum prohibitorum* was a list of books that Catholics were forbidden to read. Pope Paul VI abolished the index in 1966.

13. In Matthew, Jesus appears to disown his family: "While he was still speaking to the people, behold, his mother and his brothers stood outside, asking to speak to him. But he replied to the man who told him, 'Who is my mother, and who are my brothers?' And stretching out his hand toward his disciples, he said, 'Here are my mother and my brothers! For whoever does the will of my Father in heaven is my brother and sister and mother.'" (Matthew 12:46–50, English Standard Version).

14. Rainer Maria Rilke, "The Fourth Elegy," from *The Duino Elegies,* trans. Helen Sword, in Ralph Freedman, *Life of a Poet: Rainer Maria Rilke* (Evanston, Ill.: Northwestern University Press, 1986), 390.

15. Miguel de Cervantes, *Don Quixote,* chapter 22.

16. Berthold Brecht's "Buckow Elegies" were written at a lakeside cottage in Buckow, Brandenburg.

17. Isaac Bashevis Singer, *In My Father's Court* (New York: Farrar, Straus and Giroux, 1991), 196.

CLAUDIO MAGRIS is the author of the best-selling novels *Danube* and *Microcosms*, which have been translated into over twenty languages, and, more recently, *Blindly* and *Blameless*. He has received several honorary degrees and numerous awards, including the Prix du meilleur livre étranger (1990), Strega Prize (1997), Praemium Erasmianum (2001), Premio Principe de Asturias (2004), Peace Prize of Deutschen Buchhandels (2009), FIL Guadalajara prize de Literatura (2014), and the Kafka Prize (2016). Magris has also been a professor of Germanic studies at the Universities of Torino and Trieste. In addition to being an author and a scholar, he has translated into Italian authors such as Henrik Ibsen, Heinrich von Kleist, Arthur Schnitzler, Georg Büchner, and Franz Grillparzer.

ANNE MILANO APPEL, Ph.D., has translated works by Claudio Magris, Paolo Giordano, Paolo Maurensig, Giuseppe Catozzella, Primo Levi, Giovanni Arpino, Roberto Saviano, and many others. Her awards include the Italian Prose in Translation Award (2015), the John Florio Prize for Italian Translation (2013), and the Northern California Book Award for Translation (2014 and 2013).